# *Matsue, Japan*

## *Seven walks through seventeen centuries*

Andrew Endersby
© 2021

# Contents

# "Tell your friends!"

This is what the departing local government official said to me after we'd sat together at a bar in Matsue one evening. The location was down a side street off a popular shopping and eating area that contained dozens of restaurants and bars. I can't tell you why I had chosen this place except maybe because the sign outside was lit up in an eye-catching shade of green.

The place was small with only seven stools at the counter and a seating area with two tables behind us, but the atmosphere was convivial and even though I had chosen the most inconspicuous seat at the bar, it wasn't long before I'd become involved with the locals' discussions. The manager served drinks and maintained the conversation while bottles of sake and whisky lined up along shelves on mirrored walls behind her.

The government official was a little drunk and struggling into his jacket, arm still navigating the sleeve, as he exhorted me to help spread the word about his hometown's many charms. I promised that I would and he left satisfied, except that I was kind of lying. This was already my fourth visit and by now I had very few friends who didn't already know about my fondness for Matsue. But since I had promised, I decided I ought to do something and if there was little point in telling my friends, I may as well try to convince a few strangers and, to this end, I decided to write a book.

"*Ever arrived in a town and had the distinct feeling that something is going on and the only person who doesn't know is you?*"

That was the opening sentence in my diary describing my first day in Matsue. I had chosen the city on a whim. I had been organising a trip to Japan, listing places I wanted to go, and it bothered me that the gap between Osaka and Hiroshima was too large and I couldn't escape the feeling that this was too much Japan to watch speed by from the window of a bullet train without getting off to experience some of it.

I was searching on Google maps for somewhere in that region that looked interesting enough for a visit when my eye was caught by a couple of large lakes to the north. Wedged between these two bodies of water was a city called Matsue but when I zoomed in for a closer look I found only a blurry mesh of pixels. No Streetview, and poor satellite imagery. It felt somehow mysterious, and it occurred to me that this'd be the closest I'd ever get to visiting somewhere new and unexplored.

And so, on arrival, I was walking to my hotel when it occurred to me that the streets weren't very busy. I put this down to it being a Sunday but then I realised that, of those people who were out, the men were all identically dressed in a sort of blue and white tunic and black trousers and everyone seemed to be walking in the same direction.

I reasoned that there must be some sort of festival going on but that made no sense because the streets were so deserted and there were no signs of any actual festivities: no stalls, no street decoration, nothing.

The number of people steadily increased until they converged on a side street leading to my hotel that was blocked by a large wooden float, designed to be carried on people's shoulders, that held two large drums. The group of men were trying to lift it high enough so that a trolley could be slid underneath. I watched, not really understanding what I was looking at but I was happy to wait until the street was clear and I could continue on my way with at least part of my puzzlement satisfied: it was a dress rehearsal for a festival which was to take place soon.

Once I'd arrived at the hotel, booked in and begun unpacking, I heard some raised voices outside. I looked out of my window and I was a little taken aback by the sight of about twenty of the aforementioned tunic-clad gentlemen directly below my window, apparently calling up to me.

I quickly disabused myself of the notion that I was the person they were after, and I reminded myself that a foreign face hasn't had this kind of reaction in Japan since the nineteenth century, but the impression had already been made: I was in a city with a slightly different character than the Japanese cities that I was used to. And I was keen to find out more.

Matsue (松江, pronounced in distinct syllables: Ma-tsu-e) is the main city in Shimane Prefecture (島根, pronounced Shi-ma-ne) and is, along with the neighbouring city Izumo (出雲, Ee-zu-mo), steeped in folklore and legends. Izumo contains one of the most important shrines in Japan, while

Matsue has a reputation for ghost stories and the whole area is often mentioned in two ancient texts: *Kojiki* (古事記, Records of Ancient Affairs, written in 712) which is a semi-historical chronicle of Japan from its creation to the year 641CE and the *Izumo no Kuni Fudoki* (出雲国風土記, completed in 733), a list of places, features and customs of the area.

While no one could describe Matsue as being in the wilderness, it is too far from Hiroshima or Okayama in the south to be a reasonable destination for a day trip. I've seen Shimane referred to as "the Tibet of Japan," reflecting both its spiritual past and its physical remoteness. There's no bullet train to whisk you there in comfort and style, and the most convenient methods of transport here are coaches, local trains or toll-roads.

If you travel to Matsue by train, your eye will be lulled into a sense of serenity by a three-hour journey from Okayama through landscapes of rice fields, thickly forested hills and meandering rivers through valleys. As such, once we approach Matsue and the vistas become flatter, wider and more suburban there'll be an air of disappointment.

But then, having recently gone through a large industrial estate, your attention will inevitably by caught by the sight of a small island in a river. Little more than a small cluster of trees surrounded by water this island also hosts a grey, weathered torii gate (the distinctive gate that marks the entrance to shrines) framing a flight of stone steps disappearing up into the dark, dense foliage. This passing view, barely lasting a few seconds, sets the scene for Matsue's particular charm. After the mundane comes a glimpse of something quietly remarkable that has you sitting up and asking yourself what you've just seen.

So where to begin with this city? How to start to describe it? Perhaps the best place would be Matsue's best known and most loved location...

# *First, the lake*

Matsue sits on the Eastern shores of Lake Shinji (宍道湖 *shinjiko*), a soothing meditative presence that is the town's defining feature. Wide and tranquil, it acts like a benign, docile sea offering enough time and space to the town's inhabitants that they may, if they so choose, rest here a while and briefly replace their daily concerns with the quiet contemplation of something more permanent.

This lake is famous for its vivid sunsets and, if conditions are right, the sunset can attract large crowds of tourists and locals to admire the display. It gives travellers a precious memory, allows lovers the chance to be in each other's company without needing something to say, and lets everyone share a moment, not just with those around them, but as a common experience going back hundreds of years.

The asymmetric skyline of the distant hills that sit either side of the lake, with their shallow inclines tumbling towards each other but falling short of actually meeting, draws the eyes towards the space between them, a brief patch of horizon seemingly untroubled by land.

The water in the lake is brackish, part salt water and part fresh, such that there is the faint scent in the air as if coming from a distant sea, even though the water is lapping at your feet. A main road runs near the prime viewing spots but the grassy area leading to the lake forms an embankment so that the noise of traffic is greatly reduced to a distant drone once you are near the water's edge.

Matsue's local authorities have been diligent in recommending certain spots along the lakeside path from where the sunset is especially beautiful even though, in truth, you'd be hard pushed to find a place where the sunset looks bad. Two features of the lake are often cited as being fine additions to any view.

This first is a pair of Jizo statues. These stone buddhas are usually found in shrines wearing red bibs around their necks and are responsible for guiding the souls of children in the afterlife. But here their purpose is to protect any sailors, should their ship sink in the lake. These statues stand somewhat taller than their shrine-bound brethren, at around two and a half metres.

The waters of the lake are broken by the second recommended feature: a solitary island that lies 200m from the shore, barely rising above the surface, hosting a Shinto shrine, a torii and a number of pine trees. This is Yomegashima (嫁ケ島) and the name literally translates as Island of the Daughter-in-law, reflecting the legend of the island's origin.

The story tells of a woman who was trapped in a loveless marriage and one winter's day she tried to escape back to her home town across the ice of a frozen Lake Shinji. Unfortunately, the ice gave way and she fell into the waters below and drowned. The god of Lake Shinji saw this and, out of sympathy, raised up an island where her departed spirit could stand so she would always be able to see the lights of her hometown on the shore.

Yomegashima is curious in that it seems to be further away than it really is: a mere two hundred metres from shore. It would be pretty easy to swim there (if it were safe to do so which, apparently, it isn't) and, in fact, it is even possible to walk to it as long as you are over 160cm tall and know which way to go.

Perhaps it is the fragility that lends it this air of remoteness. It sits so low above the water and it seems to be so delicately balanced that any approaching swimmer, on pulling themselves out of the water and onto the island, might cause the whole thing to tip over, destabilised by the additional weight.

The lake shores hold one more surprise for the visiting traveller. On the banks of Lake Shinji, between the lake and the Shimane Art Gallery, is a long patch of grass land that holds various sculptures. One of these is called *"Shinjiko Usagi"* or "Lake Shinji Rabbits" and it consists of a series of twelve bronze rabbits or, more precisely, twelve depictions of the same rabbit which is hopping across the ground in a wide arc.

If you wait a while (and you may not have to wait too long) you may see a peculiar ritual acted out in which someone walks up to one of these rabbits, usually the first or second, places some small shells in front of it and puts their hands together in prayer before bowing, and finally rubbing the head or back of the rabbit. This artwork was made in 1999 by a sculptor named Yabuuchi Satoshi and, and at some undefined point after its creation, the age-old tradition of rubbing brass statues for good luck had transferred itself to this artwork too, with the addition of an offering of shells taken from the lake shore at the feet of the two Jizo statues nearby.

Before I came to Matsue, I'd never visited a place where a superstition had taken root during my lifetime. Superstitions had always been a product of an earlier age, something handed down by older generations but here was a superstition that was barely thirty years old.

Tourist information on the sculpture is sparse regarding when this began but it informs its reader that giving an offering to the second rabbit brings happiness. This, of course, raises two questions: who decided this and, furthermore, what do the other rabbits bring?

On visiting the sculpture, there is a clear halo of grassless land around the two foremost rabbits caused by the footsteps of people who have come to ask for good luck. While the first two rabbits may be the most popular, I have seen clam shells left in front of each one of them, even the last. I still wonder about what role the final rabbit plays. Does it act as a long-eared St Jude, the Patron Saint of hopeless causes, who people pray to only after every other option has been found wanting? Also, on my most recent visit, I noticed that instead of offering tiny clam shells, some people have left money: One, five or ten yen coins left in front of the rabbits or tucked into the gap at the back of the neck. Who would have thought that even requests for good luck are subject to inflation.

I've never tried the ritual myself but that's because, since I'm in Matsue, I'm already feeling pretty good about things and don't have much else to wish for. And, since I've started at the lake, let's stretch our legs and see were the shoreline takes us.

# A walk along the new coastline

The coastline of Lake Shinji has long been the subject of tributes to its beauty and tranquillity and even now, despite all the changes in the past hundred years or so, it is still touted as one of Matsue's main attractions. Quite apart from sunset (which is listed among the list of Japan's 100 most beautiful, no less) a walk along its shores is always a pleasure. On a fine day, the placid waters are dotted with fishermen catching the day's crop of seafood and the crisp wind carries with it the faint saltwater scent coming from the brakish waters.

The footpath along the eastern coast of the lake begins as far south as Nogi station but, for much of that section, we'd be accompanied by a busy main road. Instead, we'll set off from the Lake Shinji Sunset Spot, a wide set of steps leading down to the water's edge built in 2007 as a comfortable arena to sit and enjoy the sunset over Lake Shinji with Yomegashima Island set neatly in the middle distance. There is even an information board here with a map giving the best locations to view the sunset according to the time of year so that the sun on the horizon lines up with the island on the lake, effectively turning Lake Shinji into a giant sundial. This Sunset Spot also makes up part of the town's cleverly disguised flood defences, a feature that we'll see again during our walk.

At this point, we are as close to Yomegashima Island as we can be while still on dry land. This island has also had its own flood defences put in place. Photos from the end of the nineteenth century show the island as a roughly cresent-shaped patch of land barely rising above the water, hosting two or three pine trees. Now the island has been enlarged and the edges are firmly defined with stone reinforcements, a move that was unpopular with some at the time, believing that the island had lost some of its fragile beauty.

When we set off north from the Sunset Spot, before too long, we find the two famous Jizo statues we spoke about in the previous chapter. The two statues stand at around two and a half metres tall and their purpose is to look after the souls of anyone who died in the lake. The larger one is called Sodeshi Jizo and the smaller is named Sekkai Jizo. The original Sodeshi Jizo was built in the early 1600s and originally stood at the foot of Mt. Kyouko (鏡湖山

*Kyoukozan*), which is about 100m east of here in an area of Matsue once called Shodeshicho (袖師町), hence the name of the statue. The smaller, paler statue was made in the mid-1800s in Unnan City (雲南市), some miles south-west of the lake and it got its name because it initially stood in Hamanogi (浜乃木), an area of Matsue where they made lime out of clam shells from the river (Sekkai means "lime"). In the late 1800s, it was moved and stood beside the Sodeshi Jizo at the foot of the mountain which, in those days, was still on the lake shore.

After that, subsequent measures to reclaim land from the water meant that the statues soon found themselves inland, making their purpose of offering guidance to the departed souls of Lake Shinji somewhat redundant. Then, in July 1972, the statues were moved to their current location, beside the lake once again. The Sodeshi Jizo was replaced by a new statue in 1993 and, on closer inspection, the Sekkai Jizo has also had some major repair work: a crack that goes right around the neck tells us that at some point the statue must have lost its head.

As we carry on, we approach Kishi Park (岸公園) and we can see, up on top of the bank on our right, a statue of a couple of manga characters. It is called "A long day for Heita and Gatapishi" (平太とガタピシのなが〜い 一日) and it features two much-loved creations from the pen of Matsue-born writer Shunji Sonoyama. This manga tells the story about a clever dog (Gatapishi) who looks after the young boy Heita in their many adventures. The statue was built in 1998 by local artist Fumio Araki, five years after Shunji Sonoyama's death at the age of only 57. Even though I don't know the story at all, I found something poignant about the two cartoon characters looking out across the lake, fishing rod in hand, always in expectation of another adventure ahead.

Kishi Park was opened in 1999, replacing the concrete flood defences that used to stand here with something easier on the eye but still fulfilling the same purpose. It now hosts a number of sculptures as well as the Shimane Art Gallery which was also opened in 1999 as part of a regeneration plan for the area. It's definitely worth a visit but, at the time of writing, it is closed for refurbishment with a proposed reopening date of May 2022. In the meantime, it's enough to know that before the gallery, a school stood here until 1995. Nothing of that remains apart from a stone monument tucked away in the southernmost corner of the gallery's car park that has the school's motto (強く正しく, *"Tsuyoku, Tadashiku"* "Strong and Just") engraved upon it.

We follow the path round, past our friends the Lake Shinji Rabbits, and up to a small bridge over the Tenjin River to Shirakata Park (白潟公園).

The south of this park used to host an air hangar, used by seaplanes that would land on Lake Shinji. The service began in 1933 and flew to Osaka on the south coast and Kinosaki to the west. The lake was far more industrialised in the past and, before Shirakata Park was built, the lakeside here was made up of many quaysides and the area would've bustled with activity. Among these streets you would have found a restaurant where the city of Matsue itself was saved. And just here, in the park on our right up some undulating stone steps, you can find a small bust of a woman named Gentan O-Kayo who was at the heart of this episode. Her real name was Kazukiyo Nishikiori and she was the daughter of a feudal lord of Matsue, but adopted the name "Gentan".

In 1867 the Tokugawa shogunate, under which Matsue had been created, finally ended leading to the restoration of Imperial power in Japan. Although the ruling elite of

Matsue pledged allegiance to the new regime, their position was a delicate one. And so it was that in 1868 a group of ambassadors was dispatched to Matsue to check on its fidelity to the new regime. Matsue was required to pay large amounts of money and, unable to do so, the rulers of the town made arrangements to commit ritual suicide.

Meanwhile, a banquet was arranged for the visitors where Gentan O-Kayo would act as a geisha. At some point in the evening one of the officials stabbed a piece of kamaboko (a soft, steamed fish cake) on a sword and held it to her face. She calmly took the food, ate it, and asked if she could have a drink of Sake to go with it. The visitors were so impressed by her bravery that the impossible demands made of Matsue were reduced and the town leaders' lives were saved.

Keep going north past plenty of pine trees, which is appropriate since the name Matsue literally translates to Pine Tree Bay. At the northern end of the park is Shinjiko Ohashi Bridge which was built in 1972. There are a couple of covered areas along the bridge for people to stop and enjoy the sunset to the west. There are identical seating areas on the other side of the bridge. For those who want to enjoy the sunrise, I suppose.

On the other side of the Ohashi River, we take the stairs on our left down to the lake. Across the four lanes of busy traffic on our right is Suetsugu Park (末次公園), accessible via the underpass next to the stairs we just used. There's no reason to visit it unless you need to use the toilet there, but it's worth mentioning for its curious history. In the past the park was bigger, extending west to include the area where the Matsue City Hall now stands, and there used to be a cycle track. They held Keirin races in which cyclists race around a circuit with a track angled at about forty-five degrees. This arena was built a few years after the war to bring in some gambling money to the cash-strapped city. It opened on 30th May 1950 and, for a while, it was a huge success.

But the craze wore off and, since these cycling arenas were popping up across Japan, the nationwide mood turned against gambling. In Matsue the attendances fell and then, in July 1953, it was caught up in a betting scandal which seems to have been the final straw for the local government because in the following month it was closed. For a while, the now-disused steeply banked track was popular with sunbathers until, finally, it was demolished in 1956 and no sign of it now remains. The park is only half the size it was back then due to the building of Matsue City Hall. At the time of writing, there is a plan to use part of the western half as a temporary car park while the City Hall is redeveloped so, depending on when you visit, there may be even fewer reasons to take a walk through this park than usual.

A little further along our lakeside walk, a strip of greenery emerges between the main road and the lake. This is Chidoriminami Park (千鳥南公園) and it contains a sizeable monument to Lafcadio Hearn, an Irish-Greek journalist who wrote about Matsue in the late 1800s and published anthologies of Japanese ghost stories. We'll learn more about him later. Near this memorial is a statue illustrating one of the stories that he collected.

There is the figure of a seated man, playing a biwa (a sort of Japanese lute) head tilted back, mouth open, caught mid-song. This person is Miminashi no Hoichi (Earless Hoichi) and he features in a story that is set hundreds of miles away in the south-west of Japan but it became famous after Lafcadio

Hearn recounted the story in his collection of Japanese ghost stories "Kwaidan". The story is told in English on a green metal plaque beside the statue but it is somewhat weathered and pretty difficult to read. In summary, the story goes like this:

*Hoichi was a blind minstrel who was talented but very poor, so he lived in a temple. One evening while Hoichi sat alone, a samurai arrived and asked him to play for his master: a lord who was travelling incognito so Hoichi was sworn to secrecy. He agreed, and was lead by the samurai to the venue where he played all night. This happened again the next night, which is when the temple priest noticed Hoichi was not anywhere to be found on the temple grounds after nightfall.*

*The next morning, he asked Hoichi where he'd gone, but Hoichi remained silent. On the third night, the samurai came again, but this time the priest was secretly watching Hoichi. He saw Hoichi stand up, seemingly of his own accord, and walk away from the temple. He then walked into a cemetery where he would sit and play the biwa all night.*

*The following day, the priest explained to Hoichi that he was cursed and once the spirits tired of his playing they would kill him. To protect Hoichi, the priest wrote sutras all over Hoichi's body. When evening fell and the samurai arrived, he couldn't see Hoichi because the sutras rendered him invisible. All he could see were two ears floating in mid-air: the priest had forgotten to write on them. So the samurai grabbed the two ears to take back to his lord, ripping them from Hoichi's head. Hoichi remained silent and still, despite the pain, and from then on the spirits never bothered him again.*

Meanwhile, the rest of our walk has no other features other than the lake to occupy us and after about twenty more minutes the path ends pretty abruptly. We then have a number of choices: To simply turn back and enjoy the same scenery as before, only from the other direction. Or to cross the road using the nearby crossing and turn right at the 7-Eleven and follow the road west towards Matsue Shinjiko Onsen Station to catch a train to the Izumo Grand Shrine (出雲大社 *Izumo Taisha*. See the chapter Outside Matsue) or, if we're feeling energetic, we can complete a walk around West Matsue.

# West Matsue

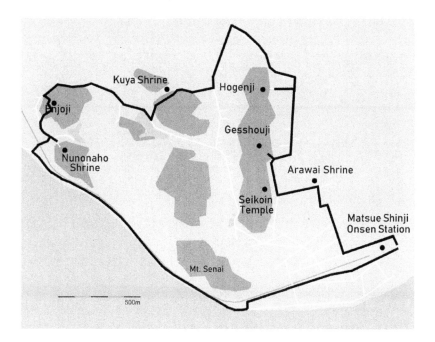

We begin at the Matsue Shinjiko Onsen train station, with its neighbouring tiny hot spring: a shallow L-shaped pool of naturally heated water, allowing you to experience the joys of a Japanese spa without getting your knees wet.

From here we head across the car park and then left once we reach the road so that we're walking with the station on our left. Carry on until the first crossroads that we come to and then turn right up a narrow lane heading north.

Keep going until the road ends at a T-junction and then go left then right again soon after that. On this second corner stands the Shokaku Temple (正覚寺 *Shokakuji*) which houses graves of two famous Edo-period sumo wrestlers, Raiden Tamogoro and his student Shakagatake who died at only 27 years old. But our first destination is Arawai Shrine (阿羅波比神社 *Arawai Jinja*), straight ahead of us to the north. This used to stand on Mount Senai (which we will pass by later in the walk) and is old enough that when mentioned in the Izumo no Kuni Fudoki in 733, the shrine's date of establishment had already been forgotten. Then, in 1562, a man named Motonari Motonari built a castle on Mount Senai while he was invading the area and relocated the shrine here. The current main shrine dates from 1814.

Turn left when facing the entrance of the shrine and you should see a tree-covered hill at the end of the road. These trees were, more or less, on the western edge of the city until the middle of the 1900s when new roads and houses were built in the wooded areas beyond.

Head this way and you'll come to a car park with a wide set of stone steps leading upwards. These take us to Seikoin Temple (清光院 *Seikoin*), the scene of a local ghost story.

*Once there lived a geisha named Matsukaze who was walking through the nearby streets when she received unwanted attention from a passing samurai. Angered at having his advances rebuffed, the samurai became violent. Matsukaze ran into the temple, hoping to escape but the samurai caught her and killed her on the steps of the main building. Despite repeated attempts to clean the blood from the steps, the stain remained and, so they say, is still visible to this day.*

Our next destination is just to the north of Seikoin Temple, so when you return down the stairs to the road, turn left and walk the short distance to Gessho Temple (月照寺 *Gesshoji*). Actually, the first temple you'll see is Torin Temple (東林寺 *Torinji*) but I know very little about this. Go through the large gate on the left, paying the entrance fee, and enter Gessho Temple, the mausoleum of seven generations of the Matsudaira family, feudal lords of Matsue from 1638 to 1871. It was originally called Tounji Temple until the first Matsudaira became lord of Matsue. He renovated it in 1664 and he enshrined the spirit of his mother, Gesshoin, here giving the temple its new name.

The grave of the 6th lord, Matsudaira Munenobu, contains an impressive statue of a large tortoise which has a stone column on its back. Legend has it the statue would walk around the cemetery at night, so the column was added to weigh the tortoise down and keep it in one place. And, truth be told, it seems to be working so far.

There is a gate to the grave of the 7th lord, Matsudaira Fumai, which is said to contain work by the famous carpenter Kobayashi Jodei, who we'll learn about during our walk with Lafcadio Hearn. Kobayashi's involvement can't be confirmed, however, and there is the curious fact that Kobayashi died five years before Matsudaira did. However, the work is of such quality and the two were such close friends that it is assumed they began work on it during Kobayashi's lifetime.

Matsudaira Fumai is famous for reintroducing the culture of the tea ceremony to Edo-period Japan at a time when it was considered irredeemably old fashioned. In fact, Fumai is his name as a tea master: he was born Matsudaira Harusato but, such is his standing culturally, he is better known under his given name than his birth name. And today, Gessho Temple has a tea room where one can look out over the gardens while you drink.

The next temple is physically right next to Gessho Temple, but will need a bit of a detour and a good few minutes walk to reach it. Return to the gate where we came in and we'll walk down the road heading west, taking the left just after the car park. Down this road, take the second left which will bring you to this next temple. This turning is easy to miss, so keep a watchful eye for a street with a set of stairs visible at the end.

This is Hogen Temple (法眼寺 *Hogenji*) which was once located on the hill where Matsue Castle now stands. It was the temple for the village of Suetsugu for about two hundred years until it was relocated, after which it burnt down and was rebuilt in such a way that the main hall now faces towards its old home, Mount Kameda.

Leave Hogen Temple by the same road we arrived, turn left to head north and then another left at the next crossroads. Follow this road as it snakes through a residential area. By now we have left the old borders of the city and until the mid-twentieth century, these roads would've been country lanes with only occasional houses for company. As we walk, we'll see occasional steps that would lead us up to small cemetery plots if you feel so inclined, and further on we'll reach a T-junction where we take a left and walk south. Once again, we're able to see a thick bank of treetops over the roofs ahead of us and, shortly after the road angles to the left, we'll take a small road heading right. Follow this to find Kuya Shrine (玖夜神社 *Kuyajinja*) which is listed in the ancient text Fudoki and is a Shinto shrine with no torii gate at its entrance. Instead, two trees growing either side of the approach act as a replacement.

If we carry on along the narrow road that brought us here, we'll come to a T-juntion with a small lake in front of us. Head right here and we're heading towards the outskirts of Matsue. Before long we'll be greeted with the sight of agricultural fields and distant tree-topped mountains. Turn left and follow the road until we reach Enkou Temple (円光寺 *Enkouji*), a little temple nestled inside a small forest.

Enkouji used to stand on the mountain where Arawai Shrine and Arawai Castle used to stand (more about the castle in a little while) but it was moved here due to water and wind damage. Once here, go past the main building on its right hand side, up to the small cemetery above. At the top of the incline on the right is a path out, down some steps and onto a road.

This is another winding road through a residential area and, after a few turns, we find ourselves at a little crossroads with Lake Shinji visible to the right. Straight ahead was can see a set of stone steps disappearing into the foliage of another hill. Up here we can find Funaho Shrine (布奈保神社 *Funahojinja*) which dates from before the 700s and enshrines Hiruko, the first son of Inazami and Inazagi, the gods who created Japan. He was a weak baby, with no bones, and so was left to drift away on a bed of reeds. It is considered by many that the god Ebisu is actually Hiruko after he'd survived this ordeal and grown older and stronger.

After this we'll return to the crossroads and head down towards Lake Shinji and then cross the railway tracks before we reach the shoreline, and the main road that runs along it. Now we turn left and return to Matsue. The main road doesn't make for a great walking companion but to the left is the hill where Tenjin Temple stands and where there used to be a castle named Arawai Castle. This castle was built by Motonari Motonari (also linked with Arawai Shrine earlier in the walk) in 1562. However, after a successful military campaign, he moved his base into his newly conquered castle, leaving Arawai Castle abandoned after only four years. These days, there's nothing left and the area where it once stood is fenced off due to a nearby rank of solar panels.

Along this road is a café if we need a rest and as we continue we may notice, visible on the other side of the crash barriers, two stone heads looking out across the lake. These belong to two jizo statues that, unlike their more famous brothers on the eastern shore of the lake, do not feature on any tourist itineraries or promotional brochures. Ever since the building of the road, it has become difficult to reach these statues and, although local volunteers try to maintain them, they have become somewhat weathered and the stonework has lost a lot of the details it once had.

Carry on and once you're past the curve in the road take the first left (if we pass a 7-Eleven, then we've gone too far). A little way down this road on the corner is a Jizo statue, the Oyukake Jizo, and a tiny onsen: a hot spring even smaller than the one at the station where we began. The water is too hot to put your hand in, but it is apparently possible to use it to cook eggs.

From here we can either keep walking along this road with the railway lines to our left for ten minutes until we arrive back at Matsue Shinjiko Station. Or we can go back to the main road and walk along the lakeside for a quarter on an hour until it guides us back into the city centre.

So we've walked along the lakeside and visited several temples, two of which were linked to a medieval and long-vanished castle. It's now time to turn our attention towards another castle. One of only twelve original castles left standing in Japan today: Matsue Castle.

# *The Castle Grounds*

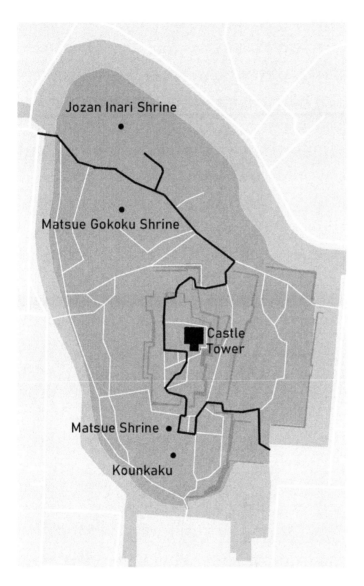

A traveller returning to Matsue Castle after two hundred years, assuming her memory is intact, would notice something very peculiar as she approached the town's most famous building. The external walls would be familiar, rising up from the greenish waters of the moat, albeit shorn of some of the greenery that once grew from between the rocks. Two black-roofed turrets perched on top of the wall peering hawkishly down at her would also be recognisable. But beyond that, she would find herself concerned at what she saw.

Visible beyond the two look-out posts, instead of a cluster of roofs, would be the gentler outlines of trees. Stricken with fear that the castle grounds had been breached and the interior destroyed, she may frantically search for any signs of the central keep (the tenshu, the tallest tower in a castle complex), in which case she would be reassured to see it through the uppermost branches of the trees.

This would bring some comfort to our returning traveller, but only a little as she entered the castle grounds to find almost all of the buildings gone and those two that remain, the two turrets on the wall that she'd seen from outside, on closer expectation reveal themselves to be modern reconstructions.

Walking through the entrance she'll be greatly affected by the missing main gate, now reduced to some slightly raised stones in the ground that mark out the foundations where the structure used to stand. There are plans to rebuild this gate except that no one is entirely sure what it looked like. There is currently a cash reward for any photo or drawing detailed enough that it'll help to make an accurate replica.

Immediately after passing this point, she will no doubt enquire as to the fate of the buildings that once stood in the park directly in front of us. There used to be a rice warehouse and sake brewery in the open space ahead of us, but those have all gone.

Now would be a good time to mention that in 1873 the Japanese government decreed that abandoned castles should be dismantled. And so, in 1875 the buildings that made up the castle complex in Matsue began to be sold off for materials. There was a local campaign to save the central keep and eventually this building was bought and preserved for the nation. But we'll learn more about that later when we go through the castle interior.

In the meantime, we'll take the stairway to our left. Hopefully our traveller friend will be reassured by the sight of a large tree next to the steps. This tree is over 350 years old and has been there since the castle was constructed. It's bound to be a familiar sight. Unless, of course, she is like me and just walked blithely past it every time without giving it a second look.

Once we carry on upwards, past the public toilets and then bear right, we'll be faced with a sight that our companion may recognise but possibly not in the place where it is now. This is Matsue Shrine (松江神社 *Matsue jinja*) and it was built in 1877 on Mount Raku (楽山 *Rakuzan*, which is in the east of Matsue, although in those days it was outside the city borders) to enshrine the former feudal lord Naomasa Matsudaira, and was relocated here in 1899.

But moving a shrine should be a concept that she is familiar with. American architecture, on the other hand, perhaps not. So her reaction to a pale blue building in the style of an early twentieth century American townhouse would be one of bewilderment. It's named Kounkaku (興雲閣) and it was built beside Matsue Shrine in 1903 when the American way was considered the height of sophistication, but now it is an ill fit for its surroundings. Not to say it doesn't have a certain charm. Like someone who has arrived at a dinner party in fancy dress, it inspires a kind of protective sympathy, born from an experience we can all share of making a brash entrance that hopelessly misjudges the atmosphere in a room. It was built to house Emperor Meiji who was expected to visit Matsue but in the end the Emperor never stayed here, although his son Prince Yoshihito did some years later. Since 1973 it has been used as a museum.

But we are nearly at the castle keep itself. Past just one more flight of steps and a ticket office. The castle is an imposing sight, even over four hundred years since it was built. This may come as a surprise to our friend since, when she left, the castle would've been in a state of some disrepair. Photographs from the late 1800s show a picture of missing roof tiles where greenery had forced its way through and ivy scaling the walls more successfully than any army had done. Now the castle is pristine, perhaps looking better than at any time since it was built.

I won't talk about the interior of the castle until the next chapter, so instead we shall meander through the park area. Since we are approaching the keep from the south, now is a good time to tell a famous legend about the castle. It is said that, during construction, the work was going so badly that they decided they needed a human sacrifice in the foundations to appease the gods who may have been angered by the fact that, to build the castle, several shrines had been moved. They found a suitable victim at a local festival, a woman who demonstrated great skill at dancing, then kidnapped her and sealed her into the walls of the castle. The building work went smoothly after that. It is said that, following this, a law was decreed that there should be no dancing in the castle grounds for fear that the mountain the castle stood on would move and the building would shake from top to bottom.

As we head past the castle, admiring its pitch-black woodwork and the gracefully curving roofs, I'll mention another threat to the castle's existence. The entire castle complex only took four years to complete which, despite legends suggesting otherwise, indicates that the work ran into no major problems.

When building the castle, they made a decision to leave a large tree stump *in situ*, even though it was within the north-eastern section of the foundations. It must have been very big, since they either couldn't go to all the trouble of removing it and its roots or they thought it was strong enough that it could support a castle. Either way, this tree stump remained as part of the fabric of the building.

Over the centuries, this tree stump started to rot away and the castle keep began to subside. By the 1950s, when they carried out the most recent renovations, the castle was sagging noticeably towards this corner; the wood panelling was warped and buckling while roof tiles were displaced if not missing entirely.

If you think that leaving the tree stump there was an appalling oversight on behalf of the builders then bear in mind that, at the time of construction, civil war had blighted Japan for over a century and castles were not the permanent fixtures that we might assume them to be. For example, only a few miles to the west stood Arawai Castle (whose site we walked past in West Matsue) which was built, served its purpose, and was dismantled within the space of four years. So, you can imagine that those building

Matsue Castle wouldn't expect it to last four hundred years.

Follow the path past the castle, through the park area and then head towards a gap in a wall that takes us down several sets of stone steps that are aged and uneven and slightly awkward to navigate. At the bottom we'll find a small pool of greenish water on our left and, to our right, a single wooden pole that seems to be drawing our attention to nothing.

The pole marks the spot of an old well. The story goes that the wall here kept collapsing during the castle's construction. On searching the well a human skull was found, pierced by a spear. Prayers were said for the deceased and the wall finally stood firm. The wall was next to a well and it was called Girigiri Well because the bottom of the well was said to resemble a whorl of hair. There really is nothing much to see, although apparently this area is haunted.

But if we leave this area with our time travelling companion and walk further down past the pond where horses used to be washed and follow the small road to the left, there are two shrines. The first, on our left, is one she won't recognise and was built to replace some tennis courts that briefly stood there in the 1930s, clearly a time when healthy recreation was more important than historical fidelity.

This shrine, Matsue Gokoku Shrine (松江護國神社, *Matsue Gokoku Jinja*) was built in 1938 and in its short lifespan it has already played a part in a remarkable piece of history. When Emperor Hirohito broadcast the declaration of surrender in August 1945, there were many listening who were appalled at this decision. In Matsue a group of dissidents gathered at this shrine on August 24 with the intention of attacking the prefectural office, local newspaper, Matsue Broadcasting Centre, the power plant and also to assassinate the governor and top public prosecutor in the hope that this would trigger similar uprisings across Japan. The prefectural offices were burned down and one person died, and the local newspaper and power plant were damaged. While they were in the Matsue Broadcasting Centre, the building was surrounded and they were arrested. This incident didn't appear in newspapers in Japan until a month after the event for fear that other people might try to emulate it.

But we'll continue on and before too long we should find a path to a forest walk on the right which we'll pass by for now. There is a red torii visible a little further along and this will be our next destination.

This shrine, Jozan Inari Shrine (城山稲荷神社 *Jouzaninari jinja*), is home to hundreds upon hundreds of small stone and ceramic statues of foxes. It was one of Lacfadio Hearn's favourite places as he passed it on his way to school. Hidden in plain sight but lost among the hordes of foxes is one statue that has a ball. It is said that a wish will be granted to anyone patient or lucky enough to find this.

Returning to the path, continuing on takes us out of the castle grounds. But crossing the moat and then turning right and walking over another small bridge takes you in the direction of the Lafcadio Hearn Memorial Museum. This, situated on the first crossroads you come to, is dedicated to the journalist and author who wrote about Matsue so poetically in his two volume work *Glimpses of an Unfamiliar Japan*. But we'll meet him properly soon. First, let's explore the inside of the castle tower that we just walked past.

# *The Castle Keep*

As mentioned elsewhere, Matsue Castle was built between 1607-1611 by Horio Yoshiharu. He was given Izumo Province (as the area was then called) by Ieyasu Tokugawa after his victory in the Battle of Sekigahara.

Initially, Horio Yoshiharu based himself in Gassantoda Castle in the city of Hirose (now part of Yasugi city, see Outside Matsue) but that castle was not fit for the latest cannon-based military techniques and so he looked around for a new venue. He and his son favoured different sites and, after his son passed away, Horio Yoshiharu chose the location favoured by his child as a way of honouring his memory.

The hill selected for the new castle already housed several shrines and the remnants of Seutsugu Castle which had stood there until 1591. The shrines were moved to new locations in town and materials from Gassantoda Castle were transported north to help build the new fortifications.

All that remains of the original castle complex are the walls and the keep: a foreboding, black-tiled scowl of a building that sits at the summit of the hill. It was never designed as a residence (the palace where the feudal lord used to live has been demolished) only as a final sanctuary in the event of an invasion. The castle has many features that make the fortress an awkward prospect for any hostile force.

The castle, from outside, has five floors visible from outside, but actually consists of six floors inside. It may be a small thing, but any chance to mislead the enemy can only be a benefit.

Should the entrance to the keep be breached, then any attacking soldiers would have to negotiate three blind corners, behind each of which would be stationed defending soldiers.

We can enter the castle with far less fuss, although we have to pause to take off our shoes. At the time of writing, after the coronavirus outbreak, it is required that you put them into plastic bags and carry them around with you. There used to be wooden lockers here where you could leave them. Whether these will ever return remains to be seen. Not that they have any historical value, but they were quite convenient.

The first room you come to after the stairs used to be a bookshop. Not during the samurai era, I mean before the virus. Now it's been cleared out and this is a recurring theme throughout the castle. When I first came here, the castle acted mostly as a museum but a few years ago someone noticed that the sum weight of all these artefacts was around five tons and could constitute a threat to the castle itself in the event of an earthquake. As a result, many of them were removed and now the main artefact on show is the castle itself. This gives a far better idea of the size and structure of the castle and various curious aspects of the building are explained by helpful multilingual information boards.

After the ex-bookshop, and past the window where you hand in your ticket, we go up the stairs to a storeroom. This contains a well that was used for water, especially in the event of a siege. Also here are two sea-green statues of fish, head down, their tails symmetrically curving upwards. These used to be on top of the roof but were taken down during repairs and replaced with new statues.

   As we ascend, there are numerous new
signs explaining the features of the castle.
Regrettably, there are quite a few
monolingual signs which have been there for
years which are mostly in the section on
Samurai armour. It's a shame these haven't
been updated especially since the armour on
display is quite impressive.

However one new addition that is very welcome is an information board about the people who saved Matsue Castle from demolition. In the 1870s, barely twenty years after Japan came out of its self-isolation, and once it had got over the culture shock of how far ahead the rest of the world had progressed, Japan was seized with a fervour for modernity and expansion. Along with this came a desire to leave behind a great deal of Japan's feudal past and this lead to the Abandoned Castle Act of 1873. This decreed that, apart from those being used by the military, existing castles should be sold off. This inevitably lead to them being demolished and this process had already begun in Matsue such that all of the buildings around the central keep had been torn down. The army controlled the castle and had been persuaded by a former samurai named Gonpachi Takashiro to leave that building until last.

When it came to auction off the keep itself, Gonpachi and a wealthy farming family Honemon were able to buy the building for 180 yen (which, I have read, was equivalent to 60 bales of rice). Following this, in 1894 the castle was repaired using public donations to save it from its perilous state.

Keep going up and once at the summit you'll be treated to views of the surrounding area, the town and lake and, to the north, tree covered hills with small neighbourhoods nestled between them.

This room has one last ghost story for us. Before we begin, a little recap of the town's early leaders.

Matsue was established by the feudal lord Horio Yoshiharu but he died before the castle was complete, aged 68. His son had already passed away, so the seat of power was inherited by the grandson. The grandson died before producing an heir so the ownership went to the Kyogoku clan in reward for their bravery in battle. But this feudal lord also died childless and the castle town was given to another clan, the third in less than 40 years. This series of unfortunately brief periods of ownership has been credited to the spirit of the young girl we mentioned earlier who was buried alive in the foundations during the building of the castle.

The next clan leader to inherit ownership of the castle was a man named Matsudaira Naomasa and one day he saw a ghost of a woman in this room at the top of the keep. The ghost told him that this castle was hers and he, thinking quickly, said that he would return it to her. The next day, he placed three small wooden pedestals in the room, with a fish on each one. The morning after this, the fish and the pedestals were no longer in the room. The pedestals were finally found in storerooms around the castle, but the fish remained missing. After this, however, the curse appeared to have been lifted and the Matsudaira family ruled over the city for two centuries.

The trick to understanding this story is to know that, in Japanese, "this castle" is "kono shiro" and that this is the same as the Japanese name for the konosirus fish, "konoshiro". It seems that Matsudaira Naomasa's deliberate misunderstanding was enough to satisfy the spirit. Either that, or she hated puns so much that she just left.

From here, there is no option other than to retrace our steps, taking care down the steep steps which won't feel very safe in just your socks.

Now it's time to meet a man who, at the end of the nineteenth century, lived near this castle and whose writings brought Matsue to the attention of the Western world.

# *Looking for Lafcadio*

When travelling abroad, one is always open to new discoveries but usually has some kind of idea about what to expect. On my first trip to Japan, including visits to Osaka, Kyoto and Tokyo, I anticipated skyscrapers, shrines, bars and complicated electronic toilets and I wasn't disappointed. When I chose to come to Matsue I had far fewer expectations but, even with that in mind, I was surprised to find constant references to a western writer that I had never heard of but who was held in such high regard here.

His name is Lafcadio Hearn (better known
in Japan as Koizumi Yakumo 小泉 八雲) and
in 1894 his book about life in Matsue was

published in the West. *Glimpses of an Unfamiliar Japan* came onto an already crowded market since it seemed that the late-Victorian era was full of travellers keen to write about their experiences in the newly-open land of Japan. But Hearn was no mere tourist. He was born to Greek and Irish parents on a Greek island and travelled constantly throughout his life. He was an experienced journalist who'd made a name for himself in Cincinnati, USA, writing about lurid murders as well as some sensitively observed commentaries on the more disadvantaged sections of society. He later moved to New Orleans and the French West Indies where he indulged his passion for mysteries and the unexplained before arriving in Japan in 1890.

Initially, he was to be a newspaper correspondent but that plan soon fell through and instead he found a job teaching in Matsue. On the 30th August 1890 at 4 o'clock in the afternoon, Hearn arrived at a quayside on the southern bank of the Ohashi River to begin a remarkable period of his life that he would remember fondly long after he'd left it behind.

He fell in love with Matsue and wrote about his time here at length in his two-volume *Glimpses of an Unfamiliar Japan*. His innate journalistic ability at describing events and cultures reached new poetic heights as he attempted to convey this new world to his readers. He covered folk stories and fables and spoke about Japan in far more depth than the diaries and observations of other itinerant writers. His Japanese wife, who he met in Matsue, helped with translations and introduced him to new aspects of the culture. In one of his chapters, he mentions a soba shop where he was told that recently a fox god disguised as an elegantly attired man ate a bowl of noodles and, after he'd gone, the money he'd paid with had turned into wood shavings. This must have left quite an impression on him: that a legend of a fox god should be so near in terms of location and time must have made him feel tantalisingly close to the sort of legends which had always fascinated him.

Anyone hoping to find Lafcadio's Matsue has one inescapable issue to address: the urban churn. The rate with which buildings are built, torn down and replaced is pretty high in Japan. This means that the school where he taught has gone, as has the inn where he first stayed and the brand new bridge whose opening ceremony he wrote about has been replaced twice since he left. Even the castle, the stoic permanent symbol of the city, has been dismantled and put back together and the cherry blossom trees around the main tower where Hearn used to take his evening walks have all been cut down.

So what, then, still remains? Where can we go to find the Matsue that so enchanted him at the end of the nineteenth century?

The most obvious starting point is the road that runs along the northern part of the moat around Matsue Castle which has been maintained in the old style of a samurai district and where it's possible to get some idea of how the city used to look.

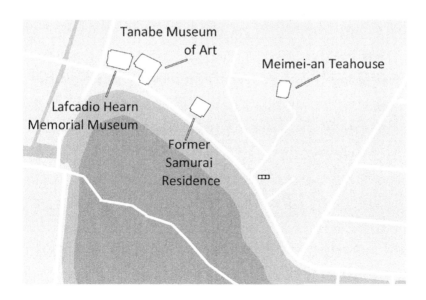

Here you can find a museum to Lafcadio Hearn and, besides that, is the actual building where Hearn lived while in Matsue. This has been kept in the same manner as during his life, including the garden that he wrote about at some length in *Glimpses of an Unfamiliar Japan*. Both the museum and the former residence are worth a visit. Also along this street are a samurai residence and the Tanabe Museum of Art which houses historical artefacts of the tea ceremony.

And on that subject, don't forget about the Meimei-an Teahouse, which is tucked away up a side road (turn away from the moat at some traffic lights and then up a narrow road until you see some stairs leading off to the left). This teahouse was built in Matsue in 1779, moved to Harajuku and then to Tokyo before returning to Matsue in 1929 before it arrived at its current location in 1966. The teahouse itself isn't open to the public, but it is the main feature of a serene area that looks out over the city and there is a modern (and far less-travelled) teahouse where one can sit and enjoy the view.

While these museums are excellent and all well worth a visit, in our search for Lafcadio perhaps we could look closer at his work. The book *Glimpses of an Unfamiliar Japan* contains an account of a walk through Matsue that fascinates with its details about the daily social events at temples, the pilgrims dressed in yellow straw overcoats and mushroom-shaped straw hats and students in uniform. In these moments, when Lafacdio takes us through Matsue, seeing Japan through his enraptured eyes, it's easy to be transported back to mid-nineteenth century Japan.

Let us take Lafcadio's walk now, keeping his text close to hand, to see how things have changed.

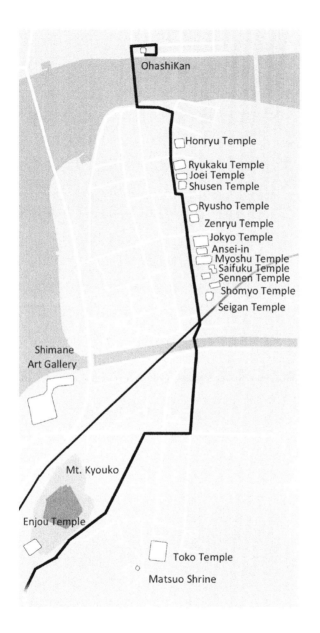

He begins on the north shore of The
Ohashi River, at the inn where he originally
stayed, named Tomitaya Inn. There's still a
hotel here called OhashiKan and, while there

is an information board about Hearn by its entrance, it has precious few links to the old inn.

He goes into some details about what he can see and hear from his window: the songs of birds, the emergence of schoolchildren and the comically loud horn on a new ship docked at the quay near his room.

After he leaves the inn, he guides us through a road that he calls "The Street of New Timber" which is the narrow road running parallel to the river on the other side of the inn. Hearn describes nets hung up on poles taller than the houses because, despite its name, the street housed fisherman. These days, the only poles here hold up Japan's complicated network of air-borne wires and cables. These do have an air of Lafcadio's *"prodigious cobwebs against the sky,"* but I suspect the atmosphere has changed considerably over the years.

Then he crosses the Ohashi bridge, admiring the mountain Dai-san in the distance to the east as he does (this part, at least, has not changed since Lafcadio's time) and he describes a very small Jizo temple at the end of the bridge which has now gone.

He writes at length about this bridge. During his stay it was rebuilt, changing from a bridge that *"curved over the flood, supported on multitudinous feet like a centipede of the innocuous kind"* to a modern iron construction

Lafcadio describes a well-known fable relating to the bridge. It states that back in the 1600s the construction was beset by difficulties and the pillars of the bridge would repeatedly be swept away no matter how many stones they sunk into the river bed as foundations. Finally, the feudal lord who was overseeing the construction of the new bridge, decided the only course of action was to have a sacrifice: a *hitobashira*, or human pillar, who would be buried alive in the structure of the bridge.

The choice was made at random: the first person to cross the bridge wearing a hakama (a kind of trouser) without a machi (a rigid board that covers the knots of the hakama at the back) would be the victim. One man, named Gensuke, crossed in this manner of attire and was swiftly made a sacrifice. According to Hearn, this lead to the bridge standing firm for another three hundred years. The middle pillar of the bridge was called Gensuke's Pillar, and a flickering red light was sometimes seen over the bridge. Hearn recounts this legend in a newspaper article where he describes in some detail the opening ceremony of the 15th Ohashi Bridge.

Hearn explains how the widespread belief in the Gensuke legend persisted to his present day: how the building of the new bridge caused rumours to circulate that a similar fate could await some unsuspecting citizen: not the first to cross it, but the thousandth. Hearn writes how the question "Has the victim been caught yet?" was commonplace among visitors as they arrived. Despite the superstition, people still flocked to the opening ceremony. Hearn guesses the crowds numbered twenty thousand and said the river was so full of boats of spectators that *"one could easily have passed the Ohashi by stepping from one to the other"*. When the ceremony was over and the bridge became open to all, there was a huge roar and the citizens of the town swarmed across it, all suspicions apparently forgotten.

Returning to our walk, Hearn guides us towards Tenjinmachi (天神町) which, he reminds us, is also called the Street of the Rich Merchants. Approaching the end of the bridge, looking south, it is directly ahead of us. The dark blue hangings with *"white wondrous ideographs"* that adorned the shops on both sides in the 1890s have gone. As has much of the energy of the area. Hearn said it contained *"the richest and busiest life of the city"* where you could find many curious temples as well as *"the theatres, and the places where wrestling-matches are held, and most of the resorts of pleasure."* This all changed with the opening of the train station in 1911 which meant goods would no longer arrive in Matsue via Lake Shinji, so instead the streets around the train station became more prosperous and Tenjinmachi slid into decline. Now this area is best known for its aging population.

We won't go this way since Lafcadio doesn't go into any real detail about Tenjinmachi in his book. Instead, we're going to take a left once we step off the bridge, past a small memorial to an engineer who died in the construction of the current bridge (more about this in the chapter "A Walk Along the Old Coastline"). There is also a long, flat roughly hewn stone here with an information board beside it. This is a musical stone of Oba which, according to the legend recorded by Lafcadio, can only be transported a certain distance. Apparently, one of the Matsudaira feudal lords (Hearn doesn't specify which one) wanted one of these stones in the castle grounds but as it was carried towards Ohashi Bridge the stone became so heavy that not even a thousand men could move it, so they left it by the bridge, where it remains to this day.

Walk past this stone and follow the road as it bends south. Now we're heading into the neighbourhood called Wadamicho (多見町) towards Teramachi (寺町 literally "Temple Town") and this is an area of the city where a line of temples stretches almost from the

Ohashi River to the Tenjin River 600m to the south. When Matsue was created in 1611, this area also served a military purpose in that the walls of the various temples would offer at least some defence against any attacking forces coming from the south-east. Hearn describes this area as *"masses of Buddhist architecture mixed with shreds of gardens and miniature homesteads, a huge labyrinth of mouldering courts and fragments of streets".* When Hearn wrote about these temples, he was struck by how children use the forecourts as playgrounds and how many of them have wrestling rings in the grounds where people can wrestle or watch for free during the summer months.

Things are a little different now, of course. While a district of temples with a history dating back to the 1600s sounds a chance to stroll through avenues of ancient architecture redolent of a vanished age, then one needs to be reminded that these temples are all still in use. The religious sites in Teramachi are pristine and, often, quite similar with black tiled buildings, a courtyard, and little else to distinguish it from its near neighbours. Additionally, Teramachi is no longer on the outskirts but is in the centre of the city, barely ten minutes' walk from the station, such that any sense of quiet contemplation can't really be sustained while walking from one temple to the next. But we'll head this way and I'll try to give a little history of the place with whatever stories I happened to have found.

The first temple we come to is on our left and is called Honryu Temple (本竜寺 *Honryuji*). This temple is more notable for what it lacks than what it has. In 2018, its 175-year-old gate had to be demolished because it had become so weak that it would be a hazard in an earthquake. Now, in its place, is a clean white wall with pillars either side of the entrance where the gate once stood.

As we continue we soon come to, on our left, Ryukaku Temple (龍覚寺 *Ryukakuji*) whose gate is a gleaming white edifice of smooth concrete (I assume). This temple houses a Buddha statue that was found floating in Lake Shinji by a sailor. Next is Joei Temple (常栄寺 *Joeiji*), which is so close that it shares the same external wall as Ryukaku Temple but whose history eludes me.

Carry on following the white wall until we come to a staggered crossroads, with the road heading south a little to our left. At this junction is Shusen Temple (宗泉寺 *Shusenji*). I mentioned before how temples would hold wrestling matches, and this temple hosted a fight between two martial artists. One was a monk, Takeda Matsugai, who was famous for his feats of strength. People would ask him to punch wooden pillars in their house, leaving behind the imprint of his fist as a mark of friendship. He stayed at this temple in 1850 and during that time he fought against Ogura Rokuzo, later to become the 11th master of the Jinshinryu school of Judo. Matsugai won by throwing his opponent into some tea plants.

We'll continue south, now walking through Teramachi itself, and we'll soon arrive at Ryusho Temple (龍昌寺 *Ryushoji*) with an information board relating to Lafcadio Hearn. It tells us that he would often walk around the graveyard here and once happened upon a Jizo statue. Struck by its beauty, he asked if it were the work of a master craftsman which, indeed, it turned out to be. This confirmed Hearn's reputation as a connoisseur of art.

The next temple along is Zenryu Temple (全龍寺 *Zenryuji*). It's records were lost in a fire, but it does have one notable feature from more modern times. In the cemetery here is the grave of Yamauchi Kakugawa, a poet who was born in the adjacent neighbourhood Tenjinmachi in 1817. He became an antiques dealer which kindled his interest in the tea ceremony and, subsequently, haiku poetry. He corresponded with a poet in Kyoto and became more determined to follow poetry as a vocation.

One day, he performed a tea ceremony for his wife as a symbolic way of saying goodbye and, three days later, left Matsue during a snowstorm. He studied in Kyoto and then Edo, before travelling north. Finally, aged 41, he returned to Matsue where he built a hermitage and taught about poetry and the tea ceremony until his death in 1894. His gravestone here carries the inscription 何ひとつ見えねど露の明りかな "I can see nothing but the light of the dew".

On reaching the crossroads, we can already see the next temple sitting on the junction, just ahead and to our left. This is Jokyo Temple (常教寺 *Jokyoji*) which belongs to the Nichiren Buddhist sect with a statue of Nichiren beside the gate as you enter.

The cemetery here houses the grave of Kobayashi Jodei, a local woodworker who died in 1813. He worked for the 7th lord of Matsue, Matsudaira Fumai, and was famous in his day for his skill. If you recall, he was the carpenter who carved the mausoleum gate to Fumai's grave at Gessho Temple (see West Matsue).

He was also an alcoholic, apparently always drunk, and even invented a wooden sake cup that wouldn't leak. One story about him describes how a young carpenter, indignant that such an old soak should enjoy the patronage of the feudal lord, challenged him to a wood-carving competition.

*Kobayashi agreed on the condition that they both carve mice. The next day, in front of several people, they presented their works. The mouse of the younger carpenter was exquisite. The fur, the tail, the ears; everyone felt that, at any second, it would twitch into life and scurry away. The mouse carved by Kobayashi, well, it looked like a mouse, but was nothing special. The young challenger was announced as the winner when Kobayashi raised an objection.*

*"Surely the best judge of which is more realistic should be a cat," he insisted and his*

*opponent, thinking it would make no difference, happily agreed.*

*So, a cat was brought in and the two wooden mice put in front of him. The cat immediately pounced on Kobayashi's mouse and the contest was definitively decided in his favour, leaving the challenger ruing his insolence and amazed at the talent that could fool a cat.*

*Later that evening, Kobayashi was out drinking when the bartender asked him why he thought the cat preferred his sculpture.*

*"Well," said Kobayashi, "his mouse was better than mine but, the thing is, he'd carved his from wood, while mine was made from dried fish."*

Following on from Jokyo Temple are several temples about which I can find little. The first two have impressive gates while the ones further south are tucked away behind shops and houses, accessible down paved alleyways.

Finally, we arrive at a junction where the railway line passes overhead. Looking to our left we can see the green roof of another temple gate. This one, the southernmost in Teramachi, is Seigan Temple (誓願寺

*Seiganji*) and was once a favourite of the Matsudaira family, famous for its opulence.

After this, Lafcadio Hearn passes over a bridge which, as far as we're concerned, is under the railway and down the road as it veers right. In Lafcadio's day this passed over the Shinedote River, but this is now called Tenjin River, and this road lead into what was then a more run down densely populated area with *"many a tenantless and mouldering feudal homestead."* These days it's still a residential area, but it isn't particularly decrepit or abandoned.

He heads south-west to his favourite soba noodle shop where he can watch the sunset over the lake but gives scant details that we can follow. If you want to head towards this area then keep going south and then right at the main road, then take the second left. We're heading towards Enjou Temple (more about this in Walking in Matsue if you want to pop in) where he visited with his good friend Sentaro Nishida on 19 March 1891. The soba shop, Kuribara Soba, once stood on the shoreline and I can't find it on any old map but there used to be a line of buildings south of Enjou Temple which would be the most likely location. Unfortunately, these days the houses there look out onto the concrete wall along the railway track, so there's no real reason to visit here now.

Meanwhile, about ten minutes' walk west from this neighbourhood there is another location that he wrote about: Toko Temple (洞光寺 *Tokoji*). He visited here in unfortunate circumstances – for the funeral of one of his students. Hearn described the interior of the main hall, with its candelabras with brass dragons and vessels shaped like deer, tortoise, and stork, but most profoundly he recounted the bell and the sound it made on this onerous day. "Peal on peal of its rich bronze thunder shakes over the lake, surges over the roofs of the town, and breaks in deep sobs of sound against the green circle of the hills."

Just south of Toko Temple is a neighbourhood that fascinated Hearn. It was, in those days, on the southern edge of the city and it was home to the *yama-no-mono*, a class of society that "*have a monopoly of the rag-and-waste paper business; and are buyers of all sorts of refuse, from old bottles to broken-down machinery.*" Due to their trade, they were considered outcasts and Lafcadio had always been attracted to the forgotten aspects of society. In the Japan Weekly Main, he wrote that

*"I was extremely surprised at the aspect of the place; for I had expected to see a good deal of ugliness and filth. On the contrary, I saw a multitude of neat dwellings, with pretty little gardens about them, and pictures on the walls of the rooms."*

This community has long since vanished, but the curious layout of the roads and footpaths remains and one still share Lafcadio's experience in which *"owing to the irregularity of the ground, the tiny streets climbed up and down [the] hill at all sorts of angles."* Tucked away in this maze is Matsuo Shrine (松尾神社 *Matsuojinja*), dating from 1801, which is dedicated to the Sake brewing industry.

After his visit to the Kuribara Soba shop, Lafcadio briefly describes his journey as he retraces his steps. On his way back over the Tenjin Bridge in twilight he passes a woman praying for her dead child, dropping strips of paper into the water below, each one with the image of a Jizo Buddha and perhaps an inscription upon it. Once back at the inn, Lafcadio describes the final sounds of the day and the *"soft Buddhist thunder"* of the bell at Toko Temple in the distance.

This account of his walk, which takes up chapter seven of Glimpses of an Unfamilar Japan, is endearing in its lapses into rhapsodic utterances over minor details. He diligently transcribes the calls of the street vendors, describes students marching past and lists any number of minutiae so banal that most people wouldn't even think to write about them but Lafcadio captures them in style so we can revisit his Matsue, sharing in his joy at every new discovery.

Hearn's life in Matsue was by no means perfect. The winter, in particular, disagreed with him. He described how two weeks of terrible weather postponed the New Year festivities and closed the Ohashi Bridge. Unable to face a second winter Hearn left Matsue in the summer of 1891 for Kumamoto in the south and, initially, the change was not a happy one. He found the locals too reserved and even the local superstitions, which had previously so delighted him, now seemed hopelessly backward. But the climate suited him and, in time, he came to appreciate his new home.

In 1894 he moved to Kobe to work for a newspaper there. In 1896 he became a Japanese citizen and took the name Koizumi Yakumo. A year after this he took a teaching post in Tokyo and lived in that city for the rest of his life.

Lafcadio Hearn passed away in 1904 of a heart attack. The renown he'd built up during his lifetime in the West was slowly undone by Japan's military expansionism which didn't sit well with Hearn's image of a quaint spiritual Japan. Meanwhile, In Japan he initially remained a largely unknown figure, even in the town he most adored. The French author Andre Bellessort visited Matsue in 1919, keen to see Hearn's home for himself, but he had to go to the local government offices before he found someone who knew where it was.

This changed in the 1920s when Hearn's work was translated into Japanese for the first time. The Japanese ruling elite were keen to spread the word about this author as an example of a Westerner who really understood Japan, and whose emphasis on old traditions and legends was an image of Japan they wished to maintain. Lafcadio would have been appalled at his work being used to support a regime that he'd despaired at during his lifetime. In his later years he became more cantankerous, disappointed at the country Japan was becoming. *"Carpets – pianos – windows – curtains – brass bands*

*– churches! How I hate them!!"* he wrote. A friend of his, Yone Noguchi, recalled Hearn had once said *"What is there, after all, to love in Japan except what is passing away?"*

These days his reputation sits uncomfortably on two stools. He could be considered as a chronicler of places and stories that most journalists wouldn't even consider and, as such, he was remarkably ahead of his time. On the other hand, he became a traditionalist, overburdened by nostalgia and spending most of his later life basing his writings on memories or old note books rather than the rapidly-changing world outside. But for all his faults he remains an important and engaging writer from the late Victorian-era who captured something of a now-disappeared Japan.

Lafcadio Hearn's last visit to Matsue was in 1897, just before he moved to Tokyo. He wrote about it for the periodical Atlantic Monthly where he explained his trepidation *"I felt curious in advance as to the nature of the impressions I was going to receive on revisiting, after years of absence, a place known only in the time when I imagined that all Japan was like Izumo."*

He visited his old house with its much-loved garden and the school where he'd taught and, most importantly, an old friend Sentaro Nishida who was suffering with the later stages of tuberculosis.

Hearn's final departure from Matsue was by steamer, departing from a quayside near Ohashi Bridge where he had first arrived. He was accompanied by Nishida despite the stifling summer weather. This would be the last time that the two friends met and Hearn expressed a pang of regret at his friend's hospitality in a letter he wrote shortly after.

*"I felt unhappy at the Ohashi, because you waited so long, and I had no power to coax you to go home. I can still see you sitting there so kindly and patiently – in the great heat of that afternoon. Write soon – if only a line in Japanese – to tell us how you are."*

And he ends the letter with a brief sentence below his signature that reads,

*"I still see you sitting at the wharf to watch us go. I think I shall always see you there."*

# A walk along the old coastline

Lake Shinji has a timeless air about it, due to the island shrine, the tree-topped mountains either side, and the fleets of fishing boats scattered across its surface. But this is a bit of an illusion, and if you're gazing out across the waters then there's a good chance that the land you're standing on has only recently reached its hundredth birthday. Land reclamation for farming and flood defence has reshaped the lake since the late 1800s but it's still worth taking a stroll along what used to be the banks of the lake. Since the coast is so often the focal point of a lakeside town's activities, by tracing a path along the old one we can find curious out-of-place buildings that used to serve a bustling coastline but are now firmly landlocked.

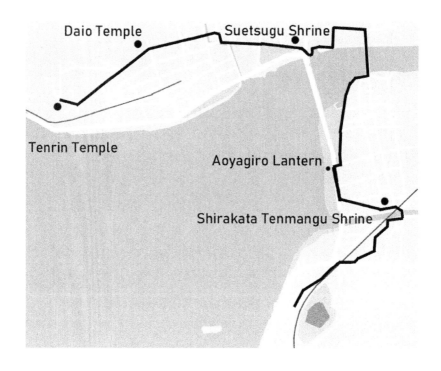

We start at Tenrin Temple (天倫寺
*Tenrinji* or, to give it its full name
Rinzaishumyoshinjiha Tenrin Temple
臨済宗妙心寺派 天倫寺) a Buddhist temple
whose cemetery overlooks Lake Shinji to the
south. In fact, the distance between temple
and lake hasn't changed a great deal over the
ages. The only additions are the railway and
North Shinjiko Road squeezing past between
the foot of the hill and the water.

The temple itself was established in 1611 by
Horio Yoshiharu (the feudal lord who built
the city and castle of Matsue at the same
time) but it wasn't until Tadataka Kyougoku

became the feudal lord in 1634 that it was moved to its current location. Then, in 1639, the fourth lord of Matsue, Naomasa Matsudaira, offered it to the Rinzai Buddhist sect and this is when it acquired its name.

The approach to the temple grounds is up a gently sloping stairway. As you ascend, to your left, you'll see a bell tower that contains a bell made in Korea, dating from the Heian period (794-1185). This bell was once housed in Hongan Temple in Izumo but Horio Yoshiharu requested it be moved to Matsue Castle to commemorate its completion. However, Noamasa Matsudaira thought a temple bell in a castle was unlucky so he donated it to the temple. There is also a cemetery here with some picturesque views over the lake.

Leaving by the same stairway we came in on, we head directly away from the temple, along a fairly unremarkable street that used to run parallel to the water's edge. But keep an eye on those car parks we're passing by. One, on the left, leads to the Daio Temple (大雄寺 *Daioji*) – the entrance is visible from the street. This temple is the scene of a local ghost story collected by Lafcadio Hearn.

*Once there was a seller of mizuame, a thick, sweet liquid. One evening a woman came to buy one rin's worth of mizuame (one rin being worth one thousandth of a yen). She returned every evening, always buying the same amount. The seller wondered why she looked so ill but when he asked, she gave no reply. Concerned, he followed her one night until she entered the cemetery behind Daioji Temple. At this point, he became scared and returned home. The next night, she returned but didn't buy anything. She beckoned him to follow her and, with some friends, he did so. She lead them to a grave in the cemetery where they could hear a baby crying. They opened the grave and found a newborn inside beside the corpse of its mother - the woman who'd been buying mizuame had been buried alive while pregnant but returned to feed her child after she died.*

Before long we cross Arawai Bridge over a river and arrive at a small junction with a triangular traffic island hosting a few trees, a tiny playground and an information point in Japanese informing any passersby that this area, Suetsugucho, was the site of one of the villages that was swallowed up by the creation of the castle town. It was an important point of entry for river traffic into the city and there was a guardhouse here once. As such, it was quite a hub of activity back in the Edo Period. Now it is much quieter, although there are two restaurants here including one named after the old village, Suetugu, where you can also buy souvenirs and gifts.

At this junction, turn right and continue until you come to another thin stream behind a crash barrier. Turn left here and carry on along the road. Before long you will find Suetsugu Park on your right, standing on land that wasn't there until the mid-20th century.  After this, the road will rise up towards a junction with Shinjiko Ohashi Bridge. This wasn't built until the 1970s so it doesn't concern us here. Instead we'll keep to the left and take the underpass. As we do so, we find ourselves next to Suetsugu Shrine (須衛都久神社 *Suetsugujinja*) whose large grey torii used to look out directly onto the lake. Just nearby stands a large lantern in the corner of the grounds which once acted as a guiding light to boats heading towards the Ohashi River. These days it's some distance from the water and it just about peeps above the hedges it stands behind.

Then, once the underpass has been crossed, there is a brief period where we are actually walking alongside some water – the Ohashi River. However, the riverside walk soon ends and we're obliged to turn inland. This detour takes us to the Kyomise Shopping Area, with its distinctive red bricked streets. Turn right along here, past a number of restaurants and cafes, and then turn right at the next traffic lights. This leads us to Ohashi Bridge, the shortest of the four bridges connecting north and south Matsue, but the longest in terms of history.

There has been some kind of crossing here since before Matsue existed and ancient records describe a bamboo bridge linking the villages of Suetsugu on the north bank and Shiragata on the south. Soon after the city was created, something remarkable occurred that meant a far more permanent structure was needed. In the late 1600s there was a flood which was so extensive that it changed the course of one of the region's main rivers. The River Hii, which is to the west of Lake Shinji, used to run into the sea but after the flood waters subsided, it now fed into the lake. This new source of water meant that the previously gentle Ohashi River became deeper and faster than before. It was after this flood that the third Ohashi Bridge was built, apparently with great difficulty and some people think that the Gensuke legend we heard about in Looking For Lafcadio is not linked to the bridge built during the city's creation, but to this third one.

Over the centuries a number of bridges have spanned this route. The current one is the seventeenth which was needed after a ship collided with the previous bridge in a storm and rendered it beyond repair.

In 1936, as the seventeenth version of the bridge was being built, a tragic accident occured. A bucket full of cement being hauled up suddenly fell and landed on the head of Kiyoshi Fukada, a civil engineer who

was working on the bridge, killing him
instantly. A copper plate bearing his portrait
is buried in the foundations 15 metres down
and a memorial plaque stands at one end of
the bridge.

To continue our walk, we turn right once
we've crossed the bridge and then follow the
road. We're now near the site of the other
village swallowed up by the new city of
Matsue: Shiragata. This was an important
location for transport heading across Lake
Shinji and Nakaumi and it was pretty large,
with a population of around one thousand
people.

More recently, but before this road existed,
this area would have had residences and
business backing directly onto the lake so
this walk would've been impossible before
the twentieth century. After the road was
built, but before the construction of the park
and the Shinjiko Ohashi Bridge currently
ahead of us, this area used to be one of the
prime spots for viewing the sunset.

Once around the corner, our first notable
location is not historical at all. Past the bend
and heading south, on our right we find the
tall, modern head office of the Sanin Godo
Bank. On the top floor of this building is an
observation room, free to enter, where you

can enjoy views of Matsue and if you time it right it is an excellent place to enjoy the sunset.

Immediately after this, we reach Shirakata Park on our right. This is reclaimed land dating from 1913 so it doesn't concern us. We'll continue along this road where once houses backed straight onto the lakeside.

We cross over the main road and continue south, noting to our right a six-metre-tall stone lantern named the Aoyagiro Lantern (青柳楼の大燈籠) which was placed her in the middle of the twentieth century. Although its location might be new, the lantern is not.

It originally stood in the neighbourhood near Shirakata Tenmangu Shrine (白潟天満宮 *shirakatatenmangu*) in Tenjinmachi, a popular area for socialising in the Meiji era. It was in the garden of a restaurant Aoyanagirou which, in those days, was on the lake shoreline and the lantern acted as a lighthouse for boats entering the Tenjin River. Due to the land reclamation program it was soon inland, shorn of its initial purpose, but it was moved to its new spot in 1958, making it a nice example of a structure that is older than the ground it stands upon.

Truth be told, as we carry on walking along this main road, we're not strictly following the old coast anymore which is about a dozen metres or so to our left.

On our left, we soon pass the NHK offices with its tall antenna sprouting up from the roof. Tucked away, by the side of the building, is a squat stone structure that you would imagine is probably a lantern. It was, however, used to play radio programs in public and it stood in the grounds of Matsue Castle from 1933 to 1995 and, I assume, was used to broadcast shows to improve the national spirit. If you approach close enough, you'll see the letters JOTK in the side of the tower. This is the call sign for the Matsue NHK radio station.

After this, we'll pass an empty lot and then hit a road heading south-east away from the park. This road takes us to the Shirakata Tenmangu Shrine. Once we reach the main road, the main entrance to the shrine is a little way to our left. This road, Tenjinmachi, used to be Matsue's main shopping area and thriving business district when there was a quay on the lakeside nearby.

The shrine is dedicated to Sugawara no Michizane (菅原道真公) who was a seventh century scholar and a poet who is now revered as the god of learning. He was a victim of political machinations during his life which saw him stripped of his title and exiled. After his death a series of disasters befell Japan and the emperor, and it was widely believed this was caused by the late Michizane getting his revenge, and so the Kitano Tenmangu Shrine was built in Kyoto to enshrine him in an attempt at pacifying his soul.

There are two statues here that can bring good luck. The first is a stone statue of the young Michizane, and opposite this statue is a brown ox, which references Sugawara no Michizane's death. The legend says that, after he died in exile in Kyushu (the large island off the south-west coast of the Japanese mainland) his body was being transported by ox and carriage when the ox suddenly stopped and couldn't be moved again. So they decided to bury Michizane nearby, and now the temple Dazaifu Tenmangu stands in that very place. This temple doesn't have anything quite so historical, but it's said if you rub the ox's head, it'll bring good luck.

Back on the main road, turn right and head under the railway track, and then go over the bridge that crosses the Tenjin River. Once on the other side, take the right, to walk along the riverside for a short spell and then take the left next to the car park. Walking down this rather anonymous back street is as close as we've been so far to the old coastline and this is where local produce was loaded up on boats. In fact, after a while, a small stream follows the road on our left. You can still see the round stones that were laid down when this wall had an entire lake to hold back and not just a quietly flowing brook.

Just after one of the open parts of the stream is a crossroads so small that you might easily miss it (and if you do, not to worry. Just carry on until you meet the main road and then take a right). At the crossroad, turn right and carry on along here until you meet the main road with the forested hill that houses Enjou Temple (円成寺 *Enjouji*) ahead of us, albeit beyond a four-lane highway. And getting across this road causes us to take a little detour (because let's not just dash across like idiots).

On this road (Japan's National Route No. 9, no less) we'll head right and walk under the railway line again. After this, there's an entrance to a subway on the right. Take this and we'll be able to cross to the south and continue on our way.

This isn't the most picturesque part of Matsue, with a large concrete overpass carrying a railway line alongside us and a busy road to our right but this area once featured a rocky shoreline sloping into the lake. Ahead of us is Mount Kyouko, the home of Enjou Temple but it's completely inaccessible from this side. In Japanese the two characters that make up this name mean "mirror" 鏡 and "lake" 湖 so it's easy to imagine, before the land to its west was reclaimed, how it got its name from people travelling across the lake and seeing this mountain's image clearly reflected in the water.

The railway used to run along the ground and, when they built it, it carved a path right through a corner of the hill itself leaving an outcrop of rocks remaining, suddenly divorced from the rest. This outcrop stood where the car park to the Seven Eleven is now, and for a time it was a common place to commit suicide. I suppose the train accelerating out of Matsue round a blind corner was a suitable combination.

This otherwise unremarkable car park holds one feature that'll lead us to the end of our journey. By the side of the pavement, standing on a pedestal next to a small pine tree, is a Jizo Buddha. As far as I can tell this is standing in the same place as the Sodeshi Jizo used to stand and watch over the shores of Lake Shinji. It's possible that when the two lakeside Jizo statues were moved, this one was built to take their place. But unlike the previous statues, this has its back to the lake and is facing towards the hill. Perhaps it is there to watch over the souls of those who committed suicide here.

From here, we can return to the lake by continuing south until the next right. This leads us to an underpass taking us across the busy highway and onto a seating area on the shoreline.

# *North east of the castle*

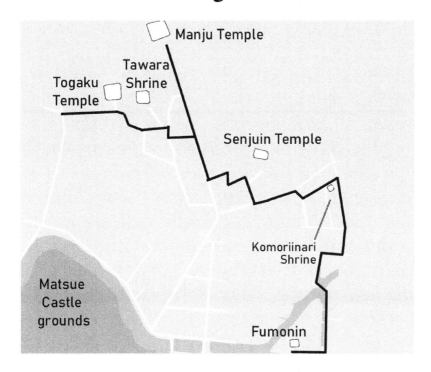

Manju Temple

Tawara
Shrine

Togaku
Temple

Senjuin Temple

Komoriinari
Shrine

Matsue
Castle
grounds

Fumonin

We begin a few streets east of the castle, next to a bridge called Fumonin Bridge (普門院橋 Fumoninhashi) looking north to the temple that gives the bridge its name. But in the past, this bridge went by a different name and, as Lafcadio Hearn informs us, there's a gruesome ghost story attached to it.

It once had the nickname Adzuki-togi-bashi, or the bridge of washing peas because a long time ago the ghostly apparition of a woman washing peas would often appear beneath it. For reasons long since forgotten, it was common knowledge that you shouldn't sing a particular song about the Japanese Iris on this bridge for fear of angering the spirit who would then fulfil a terrible revenge.

*One night a samurai, fearing nothing, went to this bridge and sang the song in full voice. Seeing that no ghost stirred, he laughed to himself and went home. There he met a tall, beautiful woman waiting for him at the gate of his abode who offered to him a lacquered box. He bowed deeply to her, but she insisted she was merely a servant passing on her mistress's gift. She then vanished and the samurai opened a box to find a child's head inside. Once inside his house he found, in the guest room, the body of his son with his head torn off.*

So we'll cross this bridge and visit the temple, founded when the castle town was built in 1611, which also hosts a tea-house called Kangetsuan. This small, thatched building dates from 1801 and is accessible for a small admission fee.

Our next destination is another temple that also dates back to the founding of the city. To reach it, leave this temple the way we entered and turn left, walking with the river on our right until we cross over another small bridge. Now turn left again so we're heading north and keep going in this direction until the road angles left, taking us over the river we've just been walking beside.

On the other side of this bridge is a curious and entirely unnecessarily awkward three-way junction. The bridge seems to be too high for the road it joins on the other bank, so there is a ramp and a sharp u-turn to be negotiated for any car drivers. This is said to be part of the town's defences: it was hoped that this would slow down any enemy army's advances.

However, our progress will be relatively unhindered, as we simply walk down the ramp and continue heading north until we hit a T-junction, go right and then take the next left. Continue up here, over another small bridge and after a while the river will accompany us to our right. At a crossroads, we'll find a small shrine to our left next to a playground that's worth noting. The neighbouring playground is apt, since this temple is called Komori Inari Shrine (児守稲荷神社 *Komoriinari jinja*) and the first two characters, 児 (ko) and 守 (mori), mean "child" and "defend" respectively and it is said the shrine got its name because here people prayed for the safety of the children of the feudal lord. It was also visited often by Lafcadio Hearn as he was fascinated by the hand drawn prayers that were pinned up there.

Take a left at the crossroads that the shrine stands at and walk west along the narrow suburban street, turning right at the end. Then take a left and then the second right, where there's a parking area and the sight of treetops above the buildings in front of us. Down this road, just as it bends to the left, is a little walkway taking us to Senjuin Temple (千手院 *Senjuin*) one of the more important and historical religious sites in Matsue.

Why it ended up here is a tale in itself. The founder of the city, Horio Yoshiharu, was given control of Izumo province and initially lived in Gassantoda Castle in Hirose (now part of Yasugi City) which is where this temple used to be. When Horio decided to build a new castle on a mountain near Lake Shinji, he brought this temple with him and placed it in a very specific location: to the north-east of the castle. The north-east section of a compass is considered the "demon gate" since whenever a demon enters a building; he or she is apt to do so from this particular direction. To protect

Matsue Castle from this, this temple was placed here to ward off evil spirits.

On the grounds of this temple is a beautiful cherry tree, two hundred and fifty years old, whose branches are held up by a surrounding wooden frame. There is also a bamboo grove to stroll around in which contains, if you can find it, a small statue of three monkeys. No one is sure of the meaning behind these. It was made in 1975 and it seems that a worshipper at the temple asked for it to be made. No one knows why but some theorise that this, too, is related to the notion of the Demon Gate: in the wall around the Imperial Palace in Kyoto, there are sculptures of monkeys in the north-eastern corner and it has been said that monkeys make good protectors because they will scratch at anything.

Retrace our steps back the way we came in. For the next few minutes, we'll be weaving through some residential streets while we head towards the next three locations, all of which date back to the fifteenth century when the city was born. When we rejoin the little road, turn right and follow it as it curves left, right and then left again until it ends at a t-junction where we turn right. Carry on up this road and before long you'll see a set of stone steps rising to a temple gate up ahead. This is Manju Temple (萬寿寺 *Manjuji*).

Once through the gate, we'll find ourselves in a courtyard of paths guiding us past carefully raked gravel areas. The pale khaki stones form ranks of lines until they meet some feature of the garden, such as a rock or bush, at which point they ripple around it. On my first visit there, this delicate formation was interrupted by a trail of small footprints left by a child who, judging by the sharp turn it took after a few steps, must have been angrily shouted at to get back on the path by their parent.

The layout of the temple seems to invite aimless wandering, as an investigation into one notable feature inevitably leads to the eye being caught by something else just a little further along.

After studying the Bell Tower beside the front gate and dawdling along the path towards the back of the courtyard, we may note, to our right, through a doorway, the sight of a row of red bibbed Jizo statues in what appears to be a small cemetery. This leads us around the back of the temple where we can admire a small garden with river and pond, take our time moving from one

Buddhist statue to the next before we find the rest of the cemetery making its way up a small hill surrounded by tall trees.

Paths allow us to pick our way up the incline, but some lead into dead ends so a little backtracking may be necessary on occasion. The more we ascend, the further back in time we seem to travel. The orderly and legible gravestones at the foot of the hill become worn by the weather and, finally, at the top they are misshapen and jostled by the tree roots growing underneath.

Once at the top, the view back down the hill resembles a river of stone, cascading down and spilling out on the flat ground below. The only sound here is birdsong or, if you arrive at the right time of day, the distant sound of children in the nearby school.

After acquiring our fill of tranquility we can descend retrace our steps down the stairs to the road that lead us here. Follow the road back south and take the second right, the one at the slightly staggered crossroads. Once you reach the T-junction at the end of this road, turn right and further on you'll see a set of grey stone steps rising up on the left.

Up here is Tawara Shrine (田原神社 *Tawarajinja*), although there are actually three flights of steps, one after the other, until we reach it. The first takes us to a car park but, despite the prosaic nature of the area, it still has a torii and two komainu - the guardian dogs who sit at either side of a torii, one mouth open, one mouth closed. The second two sets of steps are longer and flanked by not just komainu but a menagerie of animals from the zodiac, aged with moss and algae, to accompany us as we ascend to the shrine itself.

This slow climb lined by trees increases the sense of isolation from the mundane streets below, before arriving at the shrine grounds that have a surprisingly busy feel to them.

This shrine has two sections to the main hall, which is uncommon. The hall on the east is dedicated to Takemikazuchi (建御雷) the Japanese deity of thunder. The western hall is dedicated to Uka-no-Mitama-no-kami (宇迦之御魂神), a god of food and agriculture. Added to this are a number of smaller shrines lined up along the pathways. These serve to represent other, distant shrines and are miniature version of a main hall, complete with stairs and tiny shimenawa ropes across the entrance.

While some temples have an air of stillness and timelessness, Tawara Shrine feels like an important, working temple. Of course, the cars in the car park also add to that impression, but the bustling layout of shrine after shrine reminds the visitor of the amount of devotion this place attracts. Before we leave, we make sure to venture behind the main hall and down a roughly paved path into the trees to a shrine to Kōjin, the Japanese god of fire, the hearth and the kitchen.

Back down the stairs and out across the car park, when we reach the t-junction we'll turn right and take a narrow road that curves gently to the right. Before long, it'll turn back left and soon after that there's the final temple on our route.

Tōgaku Temple (桐岳寺 *Tougakuji*) is another temple that was built in Hirose in 1610, near the old castle of Gassantoda, before being relocated here in 1613. There is a sizeable cemetery on the temple grounds, and to the left of the main hall, there is a building where 500 small buddha statues dating from 1868 are kept.

Once we've left this temple, turn right and continue west along the road that we were on before. This will take us to a main road where we can turn left and head south and before long we'll be back at the castle moat.

# *South Matsue*

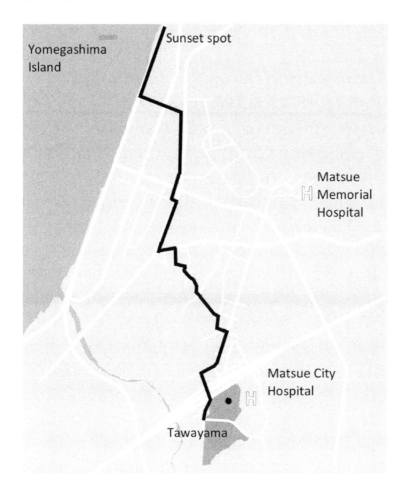

Mount Tawa (Tawayama田和山) was, for centuries, an unremarkable forested hill surrounded by fields, several miles southeast of the village of Nogi to the south of Matsue. No one paid it any attention until 1975 when surveying work was done regarding a new highway destined to go through the area. Then they found a few ancient burial mounds on the southern side, with the rest of the hill too densely forested to be properly investigated. In the end, the road was built to the north and the hill receded back into obscurity.

In 1989, however, a plan was drawn up to build a housing complex on the hill and so another, more thorough, survey took place. This found more burial mounds and a shrine site and as a result the money and time needed to survey the whole area before building could take place increased so much that the plan was abandoned and the survey ended. Instead, a nature walk was created, allowing people an educational stroll around the hill.

Then, by 1995, the city of Matsue had grown so much that its hospital couldn't cope with demand so a new location was sought. The northern part of the hill was still largely untouched woodland, and it was chosen as a likely location. In 1997 a new survey began and, after a few months, a large amount of Yayoi period (300BCE-300CE) pottery was found in what was initially thought to be a ditch. In trying to establish the length of this ditch, they discovered it ran completely around the hill and so was better described as a moat. Additionally, there were two more moats, further up the hill. If that wasn't enough, at the peak was a number of holes once used for wooden pillars. Strangely, apart from this curious structure at the top, there were no other buildings. Moats were usually built to protect a community or castle but in this instance the only thing within them was this peculiar structure which could plausibly only be religious in nature.

Once these findings became public, there were demands that the hill be maintained as an important historical site, and this only became officially recognised towards the end of the three-year survey, when the next stage of construction work was due to begin. With that reprieve, archaeological work continued for another two years and then it was turned into an open air exhibit. The current theory about the holes at the summit is that they were for a shrine with, perhaps, a shaman's dwelling nearby.

After five years of investigation, the local authorities must have been sure that they'd found everything noteworthy because, shortly afterwards, a main road was built just a few hundred metres to the south, slicing a narrow gorge through Mount Tawa.

The southern part of the hill on the other side of that new road is still covered in forest and is accessible for a nature walk. Insect sprays are recommended.

Getting there:
A bit tricky. It's a lengthy 45 minute walk from Matsue Station, so if you don't fancy that then get the bus from the station, Ichibata bus no 60 which isn't that regular – goes every two hours or so. Or it's a half hour walk from the Sunset Spot beside Lake Shinji. If, while trying to work out a route, you find yourself staring at a map then you're attention will inevitably be drawn to a feature in the layout of the city: an neighbourhood in the shape of a running track

This is all that remains of Nogi Racecourse, which was built in 1929 but was already in decline by 1935 when it was closed. After the war, Matsue started expanding south and houses started to be built around the edge of the circuit, but the area inside remained untouched. The owners of the race course only bought the land around the outside of the circuit. Inside were rice fields, which were still cultivated even during the racecourse's heyday. So the area owned by the defunct sports venue was used for building while the farmland was still active, which is how the racecourse kept its shape long after the venue had closed. It's not a place I'd recommend as a tourist attraction, but I thought I'd mention it since once you've noticed it on a map it's the kind of thing that bothers you until you get an explanation.

## *Ou Rokusha*

There are many pilgrimages across Japan designed to take people out of the usual grind of normal living and into a place of quiet dedication in pursuit of a goal, both physical and spiritual. South Matsue also has a pilgrimage which, if the walker is diligent and starts early enough, can be completed in a single day.

It is called Ou Rokusha (意宇六社, lit: "six shrines of Ou": Ou is the old name of this area south of Matsue) and it begins at Kumano Grand Shrine, some distance south of the city, and ends in Iya Shrine to the east of Matsue and it includes six shrines that date from the days of the ancient Izumo Province, before 700BCE.

The pilgrimage was popular in the 1600s when the walk would have been through dense countryside and was perhaps more of an ordeal. These days a large chunk of it takes us through the edge of Matsue, where residential areas border rice fields and it is, one imagines, less arduous than it was in Edo period Japan.

In total the journey is about 22km (13.5 miles) from first to last shrine, but there are enough distractions along the way that could well extend the walk even further.

We'll begin at the most far-flung shrine, some 10km (6 miles) south of Matsue Station.

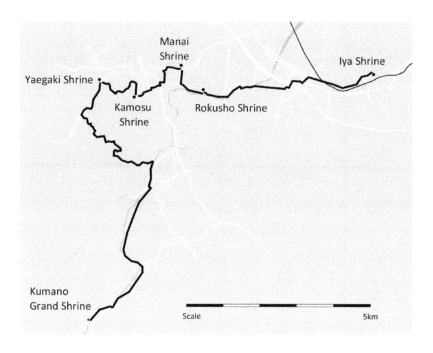

Map showing Manai Shrine, Iya Shrine, Yaegaki Shrine, Kamosu Shrine, Rokusho Shrine, and Kumano Grand Shrine. Scale 5km.

## Kumano Grand Shrine (熊野大社 Kumano Taisha)

How to get there: take the bus from Matsue station to Yakumo and then change for another bus going to Kumano Taisha on the Kumano Line (熊野線) which begins its service at half past eight.

This shrine was once equal in status to the famous Izumo Grand Shrine (see Outside Matsue), and is situated just south of the town of Yakumo. The approach to the entrance is notable for a bridge with striking vermillion balustrades along each side.

This leads us, through a torii, to the main shrine building which was built in 1948, although the shrine itself dates from 659 when it was situated on top of the mountain it currently stands beside but at some point in the Middle Ages it was brought down to its current location.

The god Susanō-no-Mikoto is enshrined here (more about him later when we talk about Yaegaki Shrine, the next location on our journey). This is also, legend has it, the place where fire was given to the gods. Looking left when you're standing in front of the main shrine, you'll see a smallish, thatched building that looks rather unkempt in comparison to the other black-tiled buildings around the courtyard. This is the Sankanden (鑽火殿, Fire Hall) where the sacred treasures of ignition are stored, until needed for sacred festivals and rites. The current building dates from 1991. The previous one, perhaps unsurprisingly, burnt down.

On 15th October the Kiribi Festival (鑽火祭) is held, when the priest of Izumo Grand Shrine visits here to borrow these treasures. As a show of gratitude, he offers mochi to the priest of the Kumano Grand Shrine who then, as curious part of the ritual, thoroughly criticises them before begrudgingly accepting them and the exchange is made. You can't help but wonder how such a unique ritual began.

The walk to the next shrine takes about two hours, has long stretches along country roads with no walkways and even throws a sizable hill into the mix. It starts pleasantly enough: As we leave the shrine, take a left at the torii at the entrance and walk along a path that follows the Iu River, which will remain on your right. If the whole walk was like this it would be well worth it, even at two hours long. But, at some point, it is necessary to cross over a bridge so that the river is on our left and from here we'll continue into more built up suburban areas, where the river meanders in and out of sight.

At this point, we are near the bus stop where we changed for the service to Kumano Taisha, so if you decide your legs aren't up to the challenge, then you can get a bus back to Matsue. Otherwise, we'll cross back over the river and before long take a left, sending us towards one of the tree-covered hills in the West.

We'll climb almost 200m and, sadly, there is no view from the top due to the dense foliage and trees lining the road. At least, once this is done, it's downhill all the way to Yaegaki Shrine.

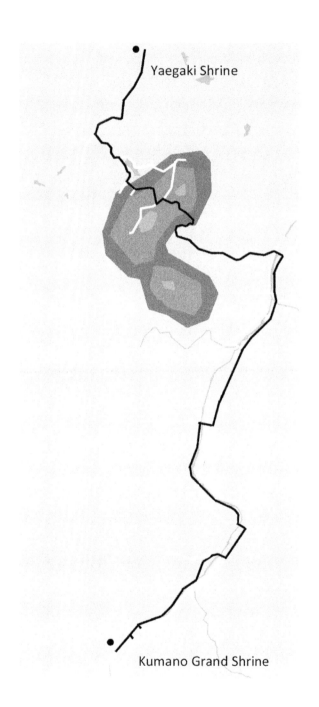

Yaegaki Shrine

Kumano Grand Shrine

## Yaegaki Shrine (八重垣神社 Yaegaki Jinja)

How to get there:

If you're not walking from Kumano Taisha and are coming from Matsue, we can get there simply enough by taking the number 63 bus from the train station and getting off at "Yaegaki Jinja." If you'd prefer to walk, it's about an hour south of the centre of town.

Yaegaki Shrine is one of the most famous shrines in Japan due to its links to marriage and matchmaking and is old enough to be mentioned several times in the *Kojiki,* the chronicle of Japanese myths and history completed in 712AD. This place is where a god, Susanō-no-Mikoto, married a princess after slaying a giant eight-headed dragon that was intent on killing her. However, if you have an image of a heroic battle between god and dragon I should probably clarify: Susanō-no-Mikoto got the dragon drunk and killed it while it was asleep. I guess the ends justified the means. Since then Yaegaki Shrine has had a reputation as a power spot for people seeking help with matters of the heart whether they're being threatened by dragons or not.

At the back of the shrine, if we just cross a road and walk down a short path, is the

Mirror Pool. This apparently has the power to foretell how quickly you will find love. Place a coin (10 or 100 yen) on a piece of paper (bought at the shrine office for 100 yen) and then float it on the surface of the water. The sooner it sinks, the sooner you will meet your soulmate. I've never tried it since I didn't want to be waiting there all day, but it's a very popular activity. The pond is very pretty in its own right, especially with the bottom lined with rectangles of paper of varying shades of green according to their age and depth.

If we return through the grounds of Yaegaki Shrinc then, from here, we can walk to another venerable shrine nearby. Just opposite the entrance is a road heading east, which we can walk or take a bike using the nearby rental service. Follow the road, as it dawdles south east and, soon after it curves north east again we'll take a right on a road marked with a sign showing directions at the junction. This is called the Haniwa Road (はにわロード) and it'll take us through a delightful little bit of Japanese countryside. The "haniwa" refers to some clay figures dotted along the way that are references to the figures found in ancient burial mounds found in the area. But more about them later.

We'll stay on this road until it runs along the banks of a small lake and then, just at the end of the lake, we'll take a right and almost immediately turn left, just after a Jizo statue. Follow this road heading north. Before too long there's a small crossroads in the path and a resting area. Take the road heading right, and keep on it as it turns south. Carry on until there's a t-junction and turn left here, following the arrow that points towards our next destination Kamosu Shrine (神魂神社). Then turn right at the next junction and walk south until we reach a car park and a set of wide stone steps on our right.

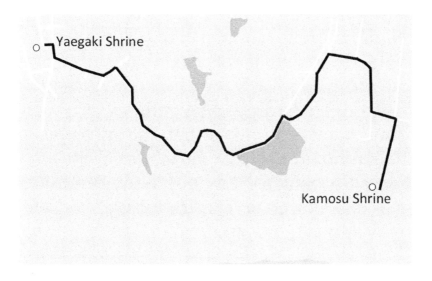

## Kamosu Shrine (神魂神社 Kamosu jinja)

How to get there:

The nearest bus stop is for the Izumo Kanbe no Sato museum (出雲かんべの里) but the service is so infrequent that it isn't much use to us. Instead, there's a bus stop on a main road: take the Yakumo service(八雲) from Matsue Station and get off at Fudoki no Oka Entrance (風土記の丘入口). There's a large map on a billboard at this junction. We want the road heading west, which we will follow until we arrive at the car park for Kamosu Shrine.

Kamosu Shrine is the oldest shrine building in Japan, with the current main hall dating from 1583, although this has been a religious site for longer than history records.

The exact date it was established is not known since it isn't mentioned in ancient texts but, according to legend, it was founded by Ame-no-homei, the ancestor of the Izumo no Kunizo (the leader of the ancient province of Izumo), and his family served as Izumo no Kunizo for 25 generations until 716.

It is dedicated to Izanami, the goddess who created Japan with her husband Izanagi. If you're lucky enough to avoid any visiting coach parties (and this is a less visited location that Yaegaki Shrine, so the chances are good) then it is a peaceful and solemn place.

The next shrine is about a twenty minute walk away although this can be greatly extended if you visit either of the two museums we're about to pass. Return to the road leading to the entrance and take a right, heading east, at the car park. The road curves to the left and on the right is the entrance to the museum of folklore, Izumo Kanbe no Sato (出雲かんべの里). This requires a decent level of Japanese to really get the most out of it, though.

Shortly after this, again on the right, is another road that leads to a museum: an archaeological museum Yakumotatsu Fudoki-no-oka (八雲立つ風土記の丘資料館) which has a permanent exhibition (in Japanese) about ancient Izumo as well as details about other archaeological sites in the vicinity with the opportunity to hire a bicycle and an audio guide (in English) for the whole area. Also, views of the surrounding area can be enjoyed from the roof.

The road we're on keeps winding left and right until it hits a main road. At this point, if you're so inclined, it's possible to get a bus back into the city centre. Just turn right and there'll be a bus stop next to the large grey building

To continue the pilgrimage, though, turn left, walk a little way and take the next right. Now we are heading out into a wide, flat, open area. The straight road is flanked on both side by rice fields with hills in the middle distance. If you enjoy the kind of Japanese films that contain scenes of thoughtful schoolchildren walking home down long, featureless rural roads then this will trigger some nostalgia, but for the rest of us it's pretty bland so we'll take the next left. (If you do want to keep going, then that's fine: just turn left at a wide road with a divide running along the middle and carry on north until the end. We'll see you at the shrine.)

Once we've turned left, it's just a case of following the road north. It'll deviate to skirt past a copse before we arrive at a t-junction. Turn right and keep going past a few houses. After a while you'll see a pale wooden torii on your left behind a stone lantern.

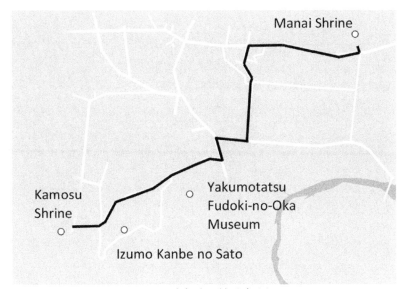

## Manai Shrine (眞名井神社 Manai jinja)

Getting there

Take the Ichibata bus to Yakumo 八雲 (departing from either Shinjiko Onsen Station or Matsue Station) and get off at Obajujiro 大庭十字路 stop. This'll be just after a crossroads with a park on the left. Then, from the crossroads, take the road east so that the park is on your left. There are the foundations of an old warehouse from the Nara period in this park. This road will take us to the gate of Manai Shrine in about ten minutes.

Manai Shrine sits at the foot of Mount Chausu (茶臼山 *Chausuyama*) and its main shrine was built in 1662, although there's a shrine called Manaisha mentioned in the *Izumo no Kuni Fudoki* in 733. Curiously, the shrine has been moved seven times since the 1660s but since records only refer to restoring and not dismantling, it is assumed that the building stayed largely intact. The deities Izanagi (who, with Izanagi, created the Japanese archipelago) and Amatsuhikone (the son of the sun goddess) are enshrined here.

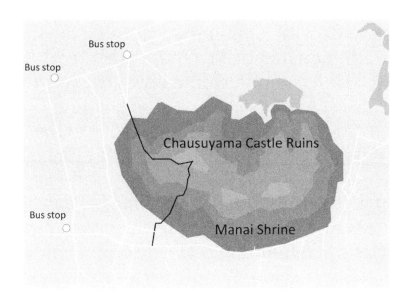

The Chausuyama Castle Ruins, which are frankly not visible at all but there's a lovely view from the peak, are situated on top of the hill the Manai Shrine stands beside. We know very little about Chausuyama Castle because it isn't mentioned in any historical records until 1717 although certain design features indicate it was constructed at the end of the Sengoku Period (1467-1615). It was probably built to protect trade, since the historical San'in route heading south from Matsue ran across the Ou Plains that the castle would have looked over.

If you want to head back into the centre from here, just head west from Manai Shrine, through some residential areas, for about ten minutes until you reach a crossroads with a main road running north to south. You'll know it's the correct road because it has a yellow line down the centre. On this crossroads is a bus stop heading north, and the buses from here go into the city centre. There are two more bus stops north of the hill but these are near schools and will be packed at certain times of day.

The walk to the next shrine is only about a quarter of an hour long. Head south from Manai Shrine along the straight road lined with pine trees. This road marks the western most border of the ancient city of Izumo Kokufu. In the 1980s, archaeological work discovered a settlement of considerable wealth and political power whose location was previously not fully understood. Since it's discovery work has continued as historians try to piece together what kind of society flourished here in the period leading up to circa 700CE. Not that you can see anything now: this is farmland, after all.

At the end of the road, turn left. Before long, the River Iu runs alongside us on the right. Keep going until you see two statues of guardian dogs on your left. This leads us to some stone steps going down and beyond that, a stone torii.

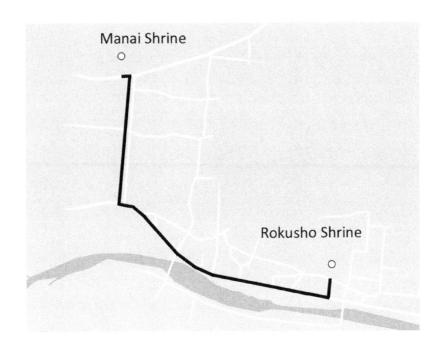

## **Rokusho Shrine (六所神社 Rokusho jinja)**

Rokusho Shrine was right in the middle of the ancient city, which could explain why six important deities are enshrined here: Izanagi, Izanami, Amaterasu Okuninushi, Susanō-no-Mikoto (all of who we've all met before), Tsukuyomi-no-mikoto (the god of the moon), and Ōkuninushi-no-Kami (the ruler of the Earthly Gods and the deity for love, marriage, among others. We'll meet him again when we visit Izumo).

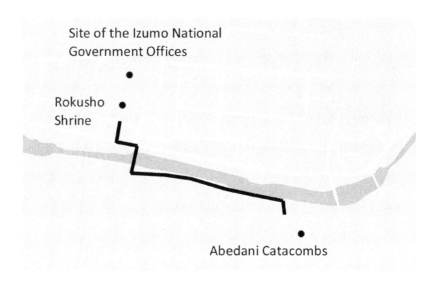

Site of the Izumo National Government Offices

Rokusho Shrine

Abedani Catacombs

## Around Rokusho Shrine

In the field immediately behind Rokusho Shrine is the Izumo Kokufu, the site where the Izumo national government buildings stood until the Heian period (794-1185). Now only the foundations remain, helpfully identified by pillars protruding upwards from the ground.

A ten-minute walk from here, across the Iu River, takes us to the Abetani Catacombs (安部谷古墳群 abetani kofungun). From the shrine, head towards the river and cross the nearby bridge. Then turn left such that you have a pine forest on your right and the river to your left. Down here, past a couple of fences that need to be shut after you've passed through them because of wild boar in the vicinity are the catacombs. There is a path that runs through the forest, up along a ridge and down again, taking about forty minutes. Scattered along this path are a number of tombs dating from the end of the sixth century. They're not catacombs in the sense of a network of tunnels, since they're each individual rooms set in hillsides, but they're pretty interesting and in a pretty woodland setting.

If you want to head back into town at this point, head south from Rokusho Shrine to the road that runs along the river and head west. Keep going until we hit a main road. This is actually the same junction we were at earlier after we left Kamosu Shrine. Turn left and just across the road, next to a large grey building, is a bus stop that'll take us back into the centre.

Having visited our fifth shrine, there is only one more to go. One that is, thankfully, near a train station so getting back into the city won't be a problem. However, it's a bit of a trek from here, clocking in at a little over an hour.

Leave the shrine and head back to the river and turn left. Follow the road as it curves left with the river and, on a clear day, you'll be able to see Mount Daisan in the distance. We'll pass two bridges, one soon after the other, and then both the river and road turn back towards the right. Once this happens, take the next bridge and then turn left, continuing east.

On this side of the river, the road doesn't follow the water for too long and soon, at a junction, we'll head away from the river and strike out between some fields. When we enter a more built up area, this road will end at a t-junction so we'll turn left, and then the next right followed by the next left. Go through the underpass and continue until a t-junction, where we'll turn right. Then at the end of this road, take a left. We're now on a main road and up ahead we'll see two overhead walk ways that we'll use to continue in this direction.

Then, at the next crossroads take a right. Follow this road for a while as it trails through industrial areas and residential neighbourhoods. Finally, after the road bears left and then suddenly goes right, we'll find ourselves walking towards a wooded area with a concrete torii gate. This is Iya Shrine. And, to be honest, we've gone so far that we've walked into the next chapter.

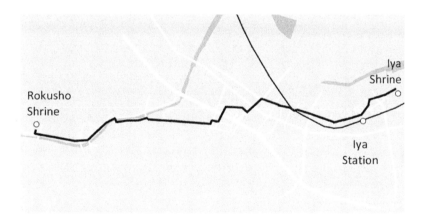

# *East Matsue*

The area in this chapter is actually a suburb called East Izumo (東出雲 Higashiiizumo) which is a little confusing until you realise it's named after the ancient province of Izumo, not the city about 40km west.

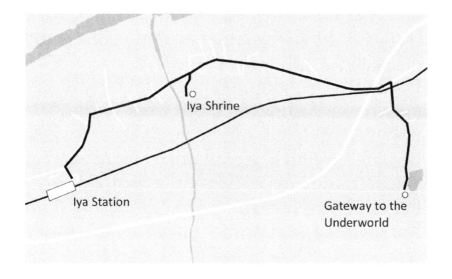

## Iya Shrine (揖夜神社 Iya jinja)

Getting there:

Take the train from Matsue Station to Iya Station. Go out past the car park and turn right at the road. Keep following this road as it abruptly turns about ninety degrees right and then carry on. After a short bridge over a stream, the shrine will be on the right.

The final stage of the Ou Rokusha pilgrimage ends at Iya Shrine. And, aptly enough, this shrine has close links to Yomi-no-kuni (黄泉の国) or The Land Of The Dead. The deity enshrined here is Izanami-no-mikoto, the god who created (along with her husband Izanagi) the Japanese archipelago and well as many deities.

Izanami died while giving birth to the god of fire and was buried on Mount Hiba, which is one of the many tree-covered peaks south of Yasugi, a little way east of Matsue. Izanami's husband, Izanagi, was very angry and lonely without her and went to the underworld to get her back. At the entrance, he met her and she explained she needed to speak to the lord of the underworld in order to get permission to return. She would do so, but he must wait at the entrance and not come in to see her. Izanagi waited but eventually became impatient. He went in and discovered Izanami's body, rotten and covered in maggots. Angry that he disobeyed her, Izanami sent the hags of the underworld to chase him and Izanagi escaped, putting a boulder into the entrance to block any pursuers.

Surprisingly, this boulder can still be visited to this day in the suburb of

Higashiizumo. It's not that easy to get to by foot, which is probably a blessing: you don't necessarily want the Gateway to the Underworld to be easily accessible. From the shrine, head east along the same road we used to arrive here until it passes under a bridge and then take the next right and keep going south until it ends at a small car park with a couple of benches. Just here, up a little embankment, is the Gateway to the Underworld.

In itself, it's not much to look at and there's no particular air of menace nor any sense of being at the threshold to another realm. There are actually three boulders beyond the stone gate with the shimenawa rope suspended across the top, and which one is blocking the entrance isn't specified. The main reason to come here is simply so you can say afterwards that you've been to the entrance to the underworld.

# *Eating and Drinking in Matsue*

Japan is famous for its cuisine and Matsue doesn't disappoint in that respect. There are two main areas for eating and drinking in Matsue, although bars and restaurants are dotted along most streets in the centre.

Of the two main areas, one is north of the station around the road Shin Ohashi Street and the other is around the shopping area known as Kyomise, just north of the Ohashi River.

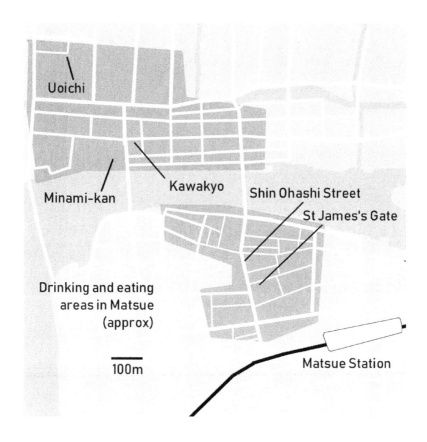

Shin Ohashi Dori was, until the 20th century, a river. But it was filled in and the city also acquired a new bridge, the Shin-Ohashi Bridge, to the north. This was only the second bridge to cross the Ohashi River and its construction in 1914 soon after the opening of the railway station was pivotal in the growth of the neighbourhood.

The pavements along the main road are covered, which is nice if it rains, and there are plenty of restaurants of every kind. And then even more along various side streets too.

If you've been to any big city in Japan then you'll be familiar with the dizzying sight of high rise blocks consisting entirely of bars and restaurants which aren't in any guidebook or website and offer no clue as to what to expect other than the sign advertising its existence. It can be daunting, trying to make a decision based solely on the name, font and colour on an illuminated sign halfway up a tower block. I asked a Japanese friend if there was any kind of code involved, something that would help a foreigner understand what they were letting themselves in for, but she said there wasn't. "You just go with your feeling," she explained. This is not such a problem in Matsue, although there are a few side roads dotted with three-storey buildings apparently containing at least a couple of bars per floor. It's probably sensible to stick to the obvious ones, such as those that label themselves "Snack Bar," "Sports Bar" or "Music Bar".

If you're worried about language barriers, then you should try the bars around the Kyomise shopping area near the castle. Most bars here have laminated sheets containing the most common phrases for ordering drinks, so you can just point to anything. Bars and restaurant with English signs outside are also a safer bet that at least some English will be spoken.

Matsue's cuisine is influenced by Lake Shinji which is part salt water, part freshwater and so it offers up a wide range of seafood. The Seven Delicacies of Lake Shinji is a course of dishes taken from the lake and it makes for a tasty and satisfying set meal, available at a few restaurants - most notably Kawakyo in Kyomise, where there is a menu in English as well as English speaking staff. You need to get there early, since my luck in getting in without booking has been a bit hit and miss, but worth it.

As for recommendations, there are plenty on the internet and I don't want to deprive my reader of the excitement of trying somewhere chosen on a whim, but one recommendation that guide books always make is the restaurant Minami-kan. This restaurant was established in the time when Lafcadio Hearn was still living here and it remains in business and in the same location to this day.

The only other restaurant still in business from that era is Uoichi Horai Kichijistuan

(魚一 蓬莱吉日庵) which was founded in 1884 and moved to its current location near the castle in 1926.

Drinking establishments in Japan tend to have two different types of tariff. There may be a set price (about 3,000 yen) where you pay the same no matter what you drink. Otherwise, there is the more familiar method of paying for whatever you buy. Matsue also has its own Irish pub if you're keen for something more familiar. St James' Gate is just off Shin Ohashi Street.

Most restaurants take credit cards these days (not so long ago, this was a rarity) but it is wise to check first. Bars, on the other hand, are almost entirely cash only. Not so long ago ago this required a certain amount of planning ahead when I first came to Japan - I once had to walk about two miles across Osaka just to get to the nearest 24hr cash point that accepted my debit cards - but these days 7-elevens and post offices have ATMs that take foreign cards. Nevertheless, be prepared before a night out and try not to get caught out with a bill you can afford but can't pay for.

# *Walking in Matsue*

Unless you're looking directly across Lake Shinji, the chances are your field of vision is framed by green, tree-covered hills. Matsue sits in a wide, shallow valley, bordered to the north and south by numerous small mountains that offer short, gentle yet rewarding rambling options. I've listed a few below.

## Central Matsue

Most rambling is done outside the city, but one small hill rises up unexpectedly out of an unassuming residential area of town hardly a stone's throw from Shimane Art Gallery. This location struck me as peculiar on my first visit to Matsue but on that occasion I didn't have enough time to investigate. On my second time here, I had not planned ahead and simply assumed it'd be easy to circumnavigate the forest on foot until I came to an entrance. Instead, I found myself sent in the wrong direction by any number of dead-end residential roads and eventually ran out of time and I had to go and catch a train. Finally, on my third visit, I had identified the correct and the easiest way on a map.

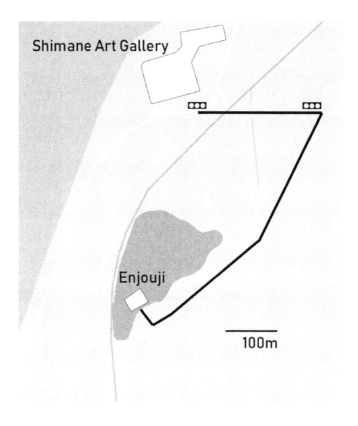

This hill is called Mount Kyouko and, on first sight, its thickly wooded flora offers no way in and it displays no reason to enter even if there was one. It merely sits there, looking as inconspicuous as a hill forest can be in a residential area, tucked behind a railway and a main road which act as two more barriers to the unwelcoming dense woodland.

But these are easily overcome and a patient explorer will do so, by heading east along the main road running past Shimane Art Gallery, and then south at the traffic lights. Following that road, one will soon find a temple at the southernmost point of the hill. This is Enjo Temple (円成寺 *Enjouji*) which has stood here since 1635 and contains the grave of Tadaharu Horio, the third feudal lord of Mastue.

The temple is flanked by two large pots full of water with a statuette of a turtle at the bottom of both. Walking around the building reveals the meticulously manicured gravel areas raked in the zen style to recreate the ebb and flow of water.

There are two entrances into the forest. One is a shallow series of steps with a bamboo fence that goes past the aforementioned grave of Tadaharu Horio, fenced off by low stone walls. The other, towards the back of the temple is a set of steps leading up and into the undergrowth.

If you take the second entrance, it is possible to be put off by a warning sign standing beside it. But it doesn't say "no entry" rather it merely insists that open fires are prohibited in this protected piece of woodland. With that established, it is a small matter of gaining access to the mysterious forest.

Just to clarify, before we get any further, that most forests in Japan possess a certain air of enigma. The Japanese landscape is around seventy per cent woodland and, while this makes for plenty of hiking opportunities, you may find yourself on a trail that is not maintained regularly. This can lead an unwary rambler into apparent dead ends, leaving them to guess which of the gaps between the trees ahead is supposed to be the path. And the tightly packed nature of these trees means that any gaps can be quite slender, while the thick foliage in the canopy of leaves above blocks a great deal of the daylight from ever reaching the ground.

In that sense, this small forest's atmosphere of mystery is quite unremarkable apart from its urban location. It doesn't take long for the forest to cut off sight and sounds of the city around it but if you come on a balmy autumn day, any sense of solitude is quickly dispelled as you'll find that you have plenty of company in the shape of mosquitoes and large spiders that build cobwebs across the path at head height. Not the faint gossamer wisps of house spiders, but thick, sticky slug trails suspended in mid-air that break with an almost audible snap and cling to you should you be unfortunate enough to walk into one.

The path is lined by stone lanterns adorned with paper strips. These contain phrases such as 南無地蔵願王菩薩 (*namu jizo o-bosatsu*) a prayer to the guardian of children. It's an affecting sight, and one that only heightens the feeling of having left ordinary suburban life far behind.

There is also a shinto shrine here, with the red paint peeling from the torii, demonstrating how closely Shintoism and Buddhism coexist. It's almost enviable how peacefully the two faiths share the same space. Before long, the path leads to a small cemetery, one which is weather-beaten and doesn't seem to be accepting any new arrivals.

Despite being on a hill, there are only a few breaks in the trees that allow a visitor to enjoy the view. Instead, the appeal is the insularity and feeling of having stepped into somewhere quite remote while still being ten minutes walk from the nearest convenience store.

## North Matsue

Getting to start of route: Take Bus from No 6 stop at Matsue Station, and get off at any of the following bus stops: the Higashi Shohokudai (東淞北台) stop, the Daini Higashi Shohokudai Danchi Iriguchi (第二東淞北台団地入口) stop or the Daini Kenei Juutaku Mae (第二県営住宅前) stop. This should take about half an hour. Walking from Matsue station takes forty-five minutes

and the route, more or less, heads straight
north from Matsue Station.

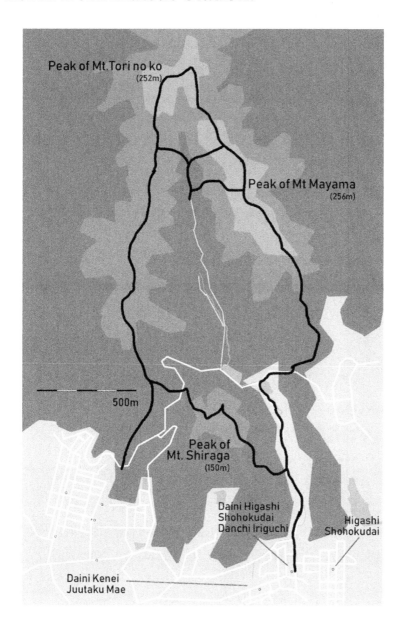

Peak of Mt.Tori no ko
(252m)

Peak of Mt Mayama
(256m)

500m

Peak of
Mt. Shiraga
(150m)

Daini Higashi
Shohokudai
Danchi Iriguchi

Higashi
Shohokudai

Daini Kenei
Juutaku Mae

The route is circular and it's up to you which way you go. Either way, it should take about three hours. Let's go counter-clockwise, since that's the direction I took.

From the bus stop, head north. Before long, we'll find ourselves on a road lined by fields and the last few houses of Matsue dotted about. This road eventually ends at a T-junction with a pond on the right. We'll turn right and it won't be long before we end up at the start of the route - a wide path leading upwards.

The first peak we reach will be Mt. Mayama (真山) which used to host a castle that, at some undefined time after it's last battle in 1571, was left to decline into disuse. Now there is precious little left to see and the main reason to come here these days is for the exercise and the views of the surrounding countryside rather than the chance to see some castle ruins.

As we walk up the slow incline, we'll be treated (if that's the right word) to incrementally higher views of the green-roofed Local Government Offices on our right. But as those buildings are obscured by trees, so the sight of Lake Shinji slowly comes into view behind us. The main thing slowing us down on this hike will not be the terrain but the desire to stop every few minutes and turn around.

The path is undemanding, although in a couple of places, it follows a ridge with slopes on either side. While still wide enough to walk quite comfortably, a little caution is advised.

The path takes us past a tombstone with the inscription 相木盛之助 更科姫墓 "The tomb of Morinosuke Aoki and Princess Soshinage", apparently the parents of Yamanaka Yukimori a famous samurai who was based in this area during the late 1500s.

Further along, after an octagonal stone structure that doesn't appear to have anything to do with the castle, we find a clearing with monument to Amago Katsuhisa. He was a member of a powerful feudal clan who, in the late 1500s, were defeated by a rival clan and he fled to the Oki Islands. On his return, he based himself in Mayama Castle from where he recommenced his battle against the rival clan until his final defeat in 1571.

After this clearing, we continue north, towards the peak Tori no Ko Yama (literally "Bird's Child Mountain") which will be written as 鳥ノ子山, 鳥の子山 or 鳥子山 depending on which map or sign you're looking at. On this path north, following a sign that points left to 寺床 ("Temple Floor") will take you down the mountain where it's possible to take a path south and head back into Matsue, ending the hike early if needs be. Otherwise our path will soon turn to the west and when the path turns again southwards, this is the second peak, Tori no Ko Yama.

From here the path heads southwards back into Matsue. There is one more peak to investigate if you're so inclined. Mt. Shiraga (白鹿山 *Shiragayama*) is only 150m tall, but it used to host a castle. Like Mayama Castle, this has also long since vanished from sight, with only some sights in Japanese to guide you to the location of certain features. This place is mentioned in one of Lafcadio Hearn's stories in *Glimpses of an Unfamiliar Japan.*

*In this tale, a physician was called to a house on this hill. He was lead there by a servant carrying a lantern and they arrived at a mansion where he was greeted with great courtesy and, once the physician had safely helped the mother give birth to a baby boy, he was treated to fine food and sent home with gifts and gold. The next day, he returned to the house in order to give thanks for their generosity but he couldn't find it: Mount Shiraga was [and still is] covered entirely in forest. He returned home and checked the gold he was paid: it was all still their except for one gold coin which had turned into a blade of grass.*

As Lafcadio Hearn explains, the family must have been an *inari* (a fox god), since a gift from a fox god always appears to be more in the night than they do in the light of the following day.

## Outside Matsue

Mt. Hongu (本宮山 *Honguyama*) is a mountain about 8 miles (13km) west of Matsue. In terms of hiking, the terrain is the easiest since it is all roads. In fact, this is the only peak that you can drive to and, at 279m high, it's the highest point in the vicinity meaning there are some great views from the top.

To get there by car, take Route 431 west. This road follows the edge of Lake Shinji and is quite picturesque in itself. Soon after a sign for Matsue Vogel Park, the lane splits into two. Stay in the right hand land and take the next right. Carry on along this road until you hit a main road running east to west. Turn left and keep going until you pass a wide junction on your right with a sign pointing to Uchi Shrine (using its other name Takanomiya 高野宮). Our turning is the one a little further on after this: a single lane heading to our right. Follow this road up and around the mountain to the peak.

To walk there, first you need to take the train from Matsue Shinjiko Onsen Station to Matsue Vogel Park Station (松江フォーゲルパーク駅) then head west until you hit a road going north and turn right and follow that road. When you come

to a main road heading from east to west,
turn left. Sometime after a wide three-lane
junction leading right, there'll be a single
lane road also heading right. Take that one
and follow the road around to the top of the
mountain.

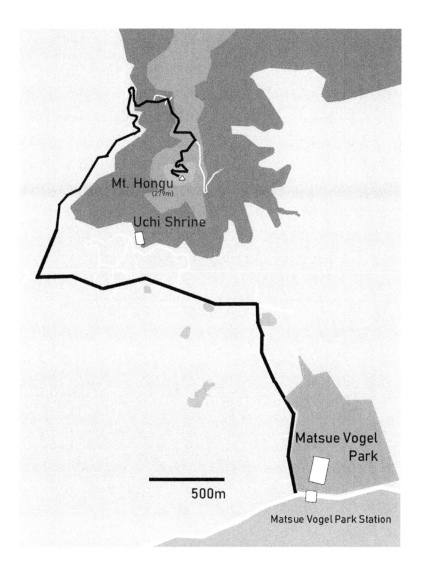

On your way there (or back), there is a shrine which is worth a visit, especially since it is only a minor detour. Uchi Shrine was originally built on the peak of Mt. Hongu in 715 when it was still called Mt Takano (which I guess explains the shrine's second name, Takanomiya), and then relocated to its current location near the foot of the mountain a couple of years later. It's a very pretty place. Unfortunately, when I visited, the weather changed to low cloud and rain so, for the most part, I was looking at things and thinking "Imagine how nice this would be if it were sunny." Even the o-mikuji (fortunes written on strips of paper) tied to a fence had wilted in the drizzle.

And while you're in the vicinity there is also, of course, Matsue Vogel Park itself, a botanical garden boasting some rare flowers in the some of the largest greenhouses in the world.

# *Outside Matsue*

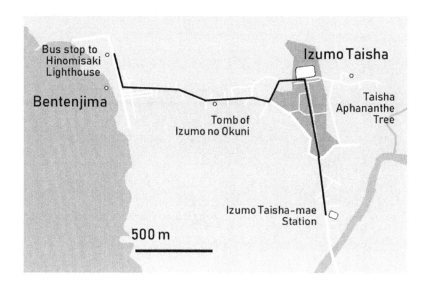

## *Izumo*

The city of Izumo, sitting on the opposite side of Lake Shinji, deserves a book of its own and it is with a sense of regret that I reduce its presence here to a few short paragraphs detailing only a few highlights.

### Izumo Grand Shrine (出雲大社, Izumo Taisha)

Taking the train from Matsue Shinjiko Onsen Station to Izumo Taisha-mae Station (出雲大社前駅) drops you on the street that leads to the second most important shrine in the Shinto religion. It is dedicated to

Okuninushi, a former ruler of Izumo and deity of marriage (among other things).

In normal Shinto shrines, when standing before the grand hall to make your prayers it is the custom to clap twice. Here, however, four claps are required: two for yourself and two for your partner.

When you leave the station, the large torii that stands at the shrine's entrance is visible to your right. This marks the beginning of a long tree-lined avenue that leads you to the grand hall of the shrine itself. Along the way there are many statues of rabbits, due to an ancient fable linking Okuninushi to the animal. In it, he and his numerous brothers were living in Izumo when they heard of a beautiful princess in the province of Inaba. They set off to ask for her hand in marriage and, being given the luggage to carry, Okuniknushi fell behind.

Once the brothers reached Cape Keta, they came upon a rabbit that had been skinned but was still alive. They told him to ease his suffering he should bathe in the sea water and stand on a mountain so the wind would dry him, and then they carried on their way. But when the rabbit followed their suggestion, the salt water caused more pain and the wind dried his skin so it cracked.

Okuninushi found the same rabbit weeping by the road and asked what was wrong. The rabbit explained that he was on the Island of Oki, and wished to visit the mainland. He came up with a trick and challenged the crocodiles to see which tribe was bigger. He asked that they all lined up in the sea between the island and Cape Keta, and that he would run across their backs and count each one. They did so, and the rabbit scampered across. But he got too confident and, just as he finished, he laughed and told them it had been a trick. The last crocodile quickly got hold of the rabbit in its mouth and stripped it of his fur as it escaped. Then he told Okuninushi about meeting the men who advised him to wash in the sea and dry himself in the mountain air, and that was the story of how he came to be like this.

Okuninushi told the rabbit to wash in a river and then roll in the pollen of the rushes that grow there. The rabbit did so and found himself restored to as before. He said to Okuninushi that, although he carries their bags, none of his brothers will be accepted by the princess and he will win her hand which, indeed, came to pass.

The Grand Shrine is a complex of buildings, the sacred dance hall is famous for its large shimenawa rope hanging above its entrance. The main hall is walled off, such is its importance but it is still an impressive sight. The area around the Grand Shrine is also full of interesting sites, such as a tall and venerated tree a short walk east of the shrine called the Taisha Aphananthe Tree (大社のムクノキ Taisha no mukunoki), which is over 400 years old, about 17 metres tall and is a shrine in itself.

## Inasanohama Beach and Bentenjima

This beach is less than a half hour walk west of Izumo Taisha, and on the way you'll pass another site of historical importance:

the grave of Izumo no Okuni. This woman, at the start of the seventeenth century, invented kabuki, a form of dance that still exists today. It's in a cemetery and, apart from some explanatory text, there's little else to see but how often do you get to visit the grave of someone who initiated a form of theatre?

Inasanohama beach is famous for its picturesque island shrine which stands on top of a largeish rock outcrop called Bentenjima (弁天島). It used to stand further out but, over time, the waves have pushed it towards land so now it sits where the sand meets the sea. It is said that around the 10th November this beach hosts deities who visit from all over Japan. They congregate here before going to the Izumo Taisha for their annual pilgrimage. This is why, so they say, in the old Japanese lunar calendar the month corresponding to November was called "The Month Without Gods" (神無月 Kannazuki) in all of Japan except for Izumo where it was called "The Month With Gods" (神在月 Kamiarizuki).

## Hinomisaki Lighthouse

There is a bus stop just north of Isanohama Beach that belongs to a service going to the Hinomisaki Lighthouse (日御碕灯台 Hinomisakitoudai). Built in 1903 it is the tallest lighthouse in Japan and offers some marvellous views once you've paid the small entrance fee and climbed its 160 stairs.

But the first thing you'll see once you get off the bus is Hinomisaki Shrine. This bright red and white shrine, is quite different in appearance to the muted autumnal shades of religious sites in Matsue. This shrine is dedicated to two gods and has two main halls: the upper one is dedicated to Susanō-no-Mikoto, the dragon slayer who married at Yaegaki Shrine. The lower one is dedicated to his sister, Ameterasu.

Along the road to the lighthouse, on the right there is another island shrine. This one is called Fumishima but, in all honesty, it lacks the aesthetic refinement of Yomegashima or Bentenjima. For a start the island itself is just a sizeable grey lump of rock and is entirely featureless apart from the shrine itself and the large number of seagulls who live, eat and defecate there. Access is prohibited apart from the priest who visits once a year on August 7th. I can't say I envy him.

The lighthouse is further on and there is also a pleasant walk in the surrounding area as well as plenty of stalls selling freshly cooked seafood.

# *Yasugi*

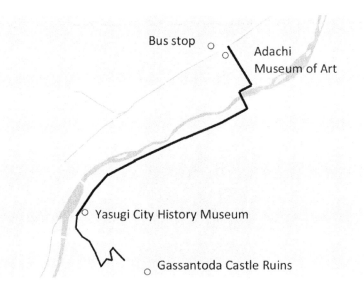

### Adachi Museum of Art
Situated in Yasugi City and founded in 1971, this art museum of international

renown is as famous for its award-winning Japanese garden than for its collection of Japanese art. A rather demure grey building from the outside, once you're inside it seems to keep going through one corridor after another, with each room offering another delightful discovery of modern Japanese art. During this, of course, you'll have occasional chances to view the tastefully arranged and manicured garden through the window or from a viewing area.

You can get there from Matsue by train to Yasugi, and then take the free shuttle bus directly to the museum (and back again). However, seats on the bus can't be reserved and in times of high demand you may have to wait for the next one. They run about every 30-40 minutes from 8:50 until 16:30 from Yasugi Station.

Opening hours 09:00-17:00, seven days a week

Entrance fee: 2,300Y with discounts for students and schoolchildren and (at the time of writing) a small discount for international visitors with passports.

## Gassantoda Castle Ruins

Built around 1396, this mountain top castle was considered impregnable and, indeed, it took almost two hundred years before it finally fell to an attacking army in 1566. Soon after this, Horio Yoshiharu was given control of Izumo Province and he preferred a new base further north and so he built Matsue Castle using some materials from Gassantoda. Unlike most castle ruins in the area, there are still visible walls above ground: certainly enough to give a sense of scale and there's a fine view from the top.

Getting there:

You can walk from the bus stop at Adachi Art Museum in about 30 minutes. There is parking at the nearby Yasugi City History Museum if you're driving.

# Accessible Matsue

Matsue is mostly built on reclaimed land. Before its creation in 1607 the area was marshland surrounded by hills and, as such, the centre of town is mostly flat notwithstanding a few steep slopes when approaching bridges. The pavements are also lined with textured pavements to allow those with sight impairments to navigate more easily. The local government has made efforts to make the centre of Matsue more barrier-free and most modern attractions are designed with wheelchair users in mind. Don't be surprised if, on arrival, a member of staff wipes down the wheels – this is simply the wheelchair equivalent of taking off your shoes when entering. By and large, the older the building, the fewer the options. The Samurai Residence has a few shallow steps to be negotiated while Matsue Castle is well-nigh impossible.

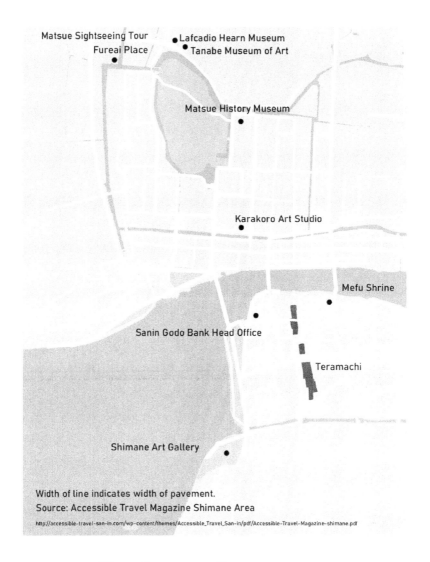

Matsue Sightseeing Tour
Fureai Place

Lafcadio Hearn Museum
Tanabe Museum of Art

Matsue History Museum

Karakoro Art Studio

Mefu Shrine

Sanin Godo Bank Head Office

Teramachi

Shimane Art Gallery

Width of line indicates width of pavement.
Source: Accessible Travel Magazine Shimane Area
http://accessible-travel-san-in.com/wp-content/themes/Accessible_Travel_San-in/pdf/Accessible-Travel-Magazine-shimane.pdf

# Art Galleries and Museums

Most galleries and museums in Matsue are barrier free. **Shimane Art Gallery**, the **Matsue History Museum** and the **Lafcadio Hearn Memorial Museum** are fully accessible although the pavements around the Lafcadio Hearn Museum are quite narrow. **Tanabe Museum of Art**, a couple of doors down is wheelchair accessible so don't be put off by the steps leading up to the entrance. The **Karakoro Art Centre**, a building of shops and craft stalls near the Ohashi River, is also accessible.

Outside Matsue, in Yasugi, the **Adachi Art Gallery** is wheelchair friendly.

## Shrines and Temples

While there are many shrines tucked away up stairways into wooded areas, there are also plenty that are easily accessible by wheelchair such as the temples in Teramachi (see Looking for Lafcadio) and most shrines in the centre. Also, there's one that I've not mentioned before but is one of the prettiest in town.

**Mefu Shrine** (賣布神社 *Mefu jinja*) sits on the riverside at the north end of the Shin Ohashi Street, known for its many bars and restaurants (see Eating and Drinking in Matsue). It predates the ancient text Fudoki and was originally on the banks of Lake Shinji, but moved her in the 13th century due to changes in the shore. The grounds are dotted with pine trees and the god of floods and tides, Hayaakitsuhiko, is enshrined here.

**Izumo Grand Shrine** (see Outside Matsue) has a flight of steps leading up to the main gate but if you turn left and follow the road as it curves right, there is a level entrance just around the corner. Once inside, the shrine grounds are mostly accessible, with a steep slope and a gravel pathway as the only potential obstacles.

**Walks in Matsue**

Of the walks I've described in this book, the following are wheelchair friendly: A Walk Along The Coastline, Looking for Lafcadio and A Walk Along The Old Coastline, even if the locations they pass by may not be.

Regarding the Ou Rokusha (see South Matsue), only three of the six shrines have roads or paths leading into the main grounds: **Kamosu Grand Shrine** (turn right at the entrance to enter by wheelchair), **Yaegaki Shrine** and **Iya Shrine** (sloped entrance is to the left of the main entrance). And if you do go to Iya Shrine, then you might be interested to hear that the path up to the **Entrance to the Underworld** is paved, if a little steep, cracked and uneven in places with a single step at the start.

## Other attractions

The **Matsue Horikawa Sightseeing Boat Tour** is a pleasant trip around the castle moat and it is accessible for wheelchair users, bearing in mind a need to book ahead and you must leave from the Fureai Hiroba Dock in the north-west corner of the moat.

The areas along the lakeside are all accessible and there is a viewing platform that is well worth a detour. It's quite well hidden, considering it's at the top of the tallest building in the area: the **Sanin Godo Bank Head Office**. At the top of this tower is a viewing gallery offering views over Lake Shinji and the town. At the time of writing (late 2021) I believe it is only open on the weekends and it closes at 17:30 or 18:00 depending on the season.

## Hiking

There is one mountain near Matsue that can be climbed by wheelchair: **Mt. Hongu** (本宮山 *Honguyama*) which is described in the chapter Walking in Matsue. Another location that is good for views is the **Hinomisaki Lighthouse** (see Outside Matsue). Although the lighthouse itself can only be accessed by stairs, the surrounding area hosts a long trail that leads you along cliff tops and through forested areas. The road leading to it is quite steep, however.

Further information regarding barrier-free options in Matsue can be found on the website http://tekuteku-matsue.com/ and, especially useful, there are pdf maps on http://tekuteku-matsue.com/useful_data.html (text is in Japanese however). A pdf brochure in English covering the whole Sanin region, not just Matsue, can be found here:

http://accessible-travel-san-in.com/wp-content/themes/Accessible_Travel_San-in/pdf/Accessible-Travel-Magazine-shimane.pdf

# *Essential Details*

## Getting there

By plane.

Matsue doesn't have an airport but two towns in the vicinity, Izumo and Yonago, both do. Izumo Enmusubi Airport (出雲縁結び 空港) is the larger of the two but there are no international flights - only domestic routes from Tokyo (Haneda), Osaka, Fukuoka, Nagoya and Oki. Yonago Kitaro Airport (米子空港) has services to and from Tokyo as well as Seoul in South Korea and Hong Kong in China. There are bus services from both of these airports to Matsue Station.

By coach.

There is a generously priced coach service from Hiroshima to Matsue that costs only 500 yen for foreigners (you must have your passport when buying a ticket, and they ask that you fill in a short questionnaire). However, the existence of this discount is reviewed every year and so how long it lasts is open to question. The coach connects Matsue Station to Hiroshima Bus Station and Hiroshima Train Station and if it still applies when you visit, it's definitely an excellent way to travel.

There are other services to and from Osaka, Kyoto, Okayama and even Tokyo but, with a twelve hour journey time, I can't recommend that last one at all.

By car.

Well, if you must. This is only really an option if you're prepared to pay for toll roads that'll reduce the time spent on the road. The Visit Matsue website ( https://www.visit-matsue.com/access/by_car ) has details about routes but they go on to say that if you're keen on avoiding toll roads then you'll need satellite navigation or to "carry detailed maps with you".

By train.

The simplest and perhaps prettiest. Take the bullet train to Okayama and then take the limited express service "Yakumo Express" from there to Matsue Station. It'll take you through some delightful countryside, so have your camera ready.

When to go

The rules about when to visit Japan in general apply to Matsue: avoid summer because of the high temperatures and avoid Christmas and New Year because of the high prices. Spring (March/April/May) and Autumn (September/October) are recommended to get the most from Matsue. October has two main festivals - the Matsue Do Gyorestu Drum Parade (whose preparations baffled me when I stumbled upon them when I first arrived here) on the third Sunday in October and the Lantern festival that is held in the castle grounds and runs from mid-September to mid-October.

No matter when you go, however, it will probably rain at least once during your visit, so take waterproofs.

# *Acknowledgements*

This is actually my second attempt at writing about Matsue. The first version written in 2019 was effectively an account of my favourite walks in Matsue in the vague form of a travel guide. My plan had been to return within a year in order to take better photos and visit those places I'd missed, but then the pandemic happened and any chance of travel to Japan went in the bin.

Instead, I carried on my research from home, combing through search results using increasingly specific terms for some pretty obscure topics.

As such, I'd like to tip my hat to the following sites

The Comprehensive Database of Archaeological Site Reports in Japan might have an English name but is exclusively in Japanese. Nevertheless, I picked my way through various search results and it was essential for the chapter on South Matsue and a pdf with extensive photographs of Matsue Castle before its major restoration in the 1950s gave me an insight into how far the castle had once declined.

https://sitereports.nabunken.go.jp/en/26
37

Then this site was instrumental in helping me understand how many castles there used to be and where they were.

https://www.hb.pei.jp/shiro/izumo/matsue-jyo/

This site has several zoomable maps of Matsue from different eras conveniently layered one over the other.

https://www.tsunagaru-map.com/pf-matsue/

This site hosts many questions about history and I frequently used it on the off chance that someone had already asked for information about the same topic that I was researching.

https://crd.ndl.go.jp/reference/

Finally, there are two books I'd like to mention.

The New Edition of Matsue's Many City Stories (my translation) 新編松江八百八町町内物語 by Araki Hidenobu 荒木 英信 is a book about the social history of the Shiragata and Suetsugu areas of Matsue. I got it near the end of writing this book, so only used it to fill in some gaps, but it is comprehensive enough that I could have spent another year researching the stories it contained.

And the photobook "Matsue" by Ueda Shoji which came back into print in 2014 is a collection of photographs of the city from 1960 and I found it helped me get a sense of how the town looked before some of the more recent additions to the skyline.

Finally, a huge amount of thanks must go to my Japanese teacher, Saori Hawker, who's patiently guided me through a lot of texts about the history, geography and folk lore of Matsue.

Printed in Great Britain
by Amazon